# THE UP SIDE OF BEING DOWN

## A Simple Guide for Healing Negativity with Mind Fitness

### Joy L. Watson

Author of *FROM STRESS TO SANITY*
Co-author of *THE MIND FITNESS PROGRAM FOR ESTEEM AND EXCELLENCE FOR CHILDREN*

| Library of Congress Number: | | 00-191870 |
|---|---|---|
| ISBN #: | Hardcover | 0-7388-3377-0 |
| | Softcover | 0-7388-3378-9 |

This book was printed in the United States of America.

To order additional copies of this book, contact:
Xlibris Corporation
1-888-7-XLIBRIS
www.Xlibris.com
Orders@Xlibris.com

# QUESTIONS

Do you sometimes feel like someone who ...
- feels generally discontented and irritated
- has bouts of depression filled with frustration
- too often takes a defensive position toward things
- makes cynical or biting remarks
- finds it difficult to embrace new ideas or changes
- often feels stressed or angry
- exhibits inappropriate reactionary responses
- is fearful of what will happen in the future
- generally exhibits low energy and critical attitudes?

If you want to ...
- nurture a warmer, more confident and generous relationship with yourself
- enhance the depth and quality of your relationships with loved ones, friends, and coworkers
- enjoy a greater sense of accomplishment in your work, community, and creative lives
- live more optimally in any area on which you focus your mental thoughts: health, education, sports, prosperity, arts, love, relationships ...

This book is for you.

**In this book, we explore a very common problem—personal negativity—and look at where this thinking pattern and attitude may come from and how it may affect our lives.**

Through identification and acceptance of your own forms of personal negativity, your focus shifts from external to internal. You begin to work to replace automatic thinking patterns with more self-directed and empowered choices. The Mind Fitness program guides your daily mental care, focusing on optimal health and well-being.

# CONTENTS

## PART ONE
## IDENTIFICATION AND ACCEPTANCE

### Chapter 1: INTRODUCTION

### Chapter 2: MIND FITNESS

### Chapter 3: WE BECOME WHAT WE IMAGE

# Chapter 4: THE BEGINNINGS

# Chapter 5: SYMPTOMS AND PAYOFFS

# Chapter 6: GETTING READY

# PART TWO
# MIND FITNESS FOR HEALING

## Chapter 7: MAGIC WORD #1: RELAXATION

## Chapter 8: MAGIC WORD #2: VISUALIZATION

## Chapter 9: MAGIC WORD #3: AFFIRMATION

## Chapter 10: RHYTHM AND STYLE

## Chapter 11: A DAILY WORKOUT

# PART THREE
# BUILDING STEADY ATTITUDES

## Chapter 12: IMAGES AND TECHNIQUES: POSITIVE MOMENTUM

## Chapter 13 BUILDING STEADY ATTITUDES: MORE TECHNIQUES

# DEDICATION
To all those who feel and challenge these feelings

# FOREWORD

Millions of people are trapped in a downward spiral of depression, anger, bitterness, and reactivity. Personal negativity has grown to such proportions it can now be considered an attitudinal addiction. Since cognition and attitude have become widely recognized as critical factors underlying health, this pervasive negativity clearly undermines our personal and collective health. Lives are cut short, careers are stunted, and relationships wither, because of negativity.

But there is an upside to the bad attitude trap. By using the right tools, you can find a way out, and experience more vitality and happiness than ever seemed possible.

*The Up Side of Being Down* is a simple guide for healing personal negativity. It offers a look at a painful condition that has become as pervasive as Prozac, and as insidious as toxic waste. The recommendations in this book will help you identify, accept, and heal dysfunctional attitudinal conditions, using a self-guided approach called Mind Fitness.

Mind Fitness, like physical fitness, is a lifestyle that leads to better health and greater fulfillment. Instead of barbells and running shoes, Mind Fitness applies the tools of relaxation, proactive reflection and whole-brain learning to create a mental and emotional fitness that promotes lasting joy and well-being.

The Mind Fitness approach embraces the principles of attitudinal healing, offering solutions for the problems of human health and well-being. The challenge of facing our own negativity—both personally and collectively—plays a large part in the beginning of this new millennium. Mind Fitness is a timely and far-reaching mental health approach to help us do just that.

# *INSPIRATION*

If there is light in the soul,
There will be beauty in the person.
If there is beauty in the person,
There will be harmony in the house.
If there is harmony in the house,
There will be order in the nation.
If there is order in the nation,
There will be peace in the world.

*Ancient Chinese Proverb*

# PART ONE

## IDENTIFICATION AND ACCEPTANCE

# Chapter 1

## *INTRODUCTION*

"My life looks great on paper. I have a wonderful
family, a fine job, and good health. I should be
happy, but much of the time I feel depressed and
out of control. Something is always wrong—at home
or at work. Lately, life seems to be one irritation
after another; something to be gotten through,
rather than enjoyed."

This 35-year-old legal secretary and mother of two teens
speaks for millions of men and women. Their lives are basically good. Their jobs are fine. They love the people around
them. They look just fine from the outside, but they're not
as happy, satisfied, or at peace as they would like to be. They
have the feeling that something is very wrong, and they are
not quite sure what it is.

They may experience waves of cynicism or pessimism
sweeping over them "for no good reason." They may either
withdraw, or lash out and say things they wish they hadn't
said. They feel stressed and frustrated. There is an inconsis-
tency in their responses. They feel out of balance. They are
unduly hard on themselves, expecting only perfection. They
don't really trust themselves or believe that they have the
power to shape their own lives. They often feel defeated
even before they begin. Sound familiar?

This cycle of negative feelings in all its many forms—

fear, depression, anxiety, feelings of being overwhelmed or defeated, anger, pessimism, powerlessness, or anything that consistently prevents people from enjoying life—tends to feed on itself. It can be so subtle that we hardly recognize it, so insidious that we begin to think it's really just the way we are. It takes so many different forms that it's difficult to pinpoint the problem exactly. Sometimes we wonder, "Is there really a problem or is this the way life is?" We just aren't sure. It's like having a persistent infection, a constant irritation that keeps us from feeling energetic, enthusiastic, and at peace with ourselves.

We don't know what to do about it. We don't even know what to *call* the problem. This book names Personal Negativity as a mental health and attitudinal "dis-ease," and offers specific solutions to reverse the cycle of painful and debilitating feelings often associated with an illness. The healing of the predominantly negative slant on life takes place as we learn to use our conscious minds constructively, appreciate ourselves and others more, and begin to take control of our future attitudes and actions.

Here are some of the truths we've identified about personal forms of negative thinking:

- They may begin early in life.
- They often grow into reactionary habit patterns during the teen years, shaping the personality and thinking patterns.
- They are a learned pattern of fearful perceptions, and reactive thoughts and behaviors, which feed and build on themselves, growing into an overall life attitude of emotional defense and protection.
- Because so many situations and people are seen through "gray-colored glasses," this condition drains energy and robs us of pleasure and happiness.

- Attitudes are contagious and pervasive, affecting others' perceptions and responses. An overall defensive, unpredictable, and reactionary attitude contaminates the social climate.
- The Up Side of this unhappy situation is that we can reverse and heal personal negativity with straightforward, powerful techniques that have proven effective in athletics, business, education, and health.
- We can learn to build positive attitudes, achieve goals, tap creative potential, and become happier, healthier, more productive people.

The approach is Mind Fitness. It is a mental health training approach—a conscious way of thinking about how you want to live your life—with daily mental adjustments that do for the mind and soul what physical exercise does for the body. Mind Fitness work is entirely internal, invisible, and subjective. We are the only ones who know our attitudes and what we really value in life. We are the only ones who can direct our own personal reactions, attitudes, and thinking.

Over the past twenty years, we have discovered that optimal performance in any field incorporates three basic skills: *relaxation, visualization, and affirmation.* These are the cornerstones of a Mind Fitness practice-training. Until now, many of us may have been unknowingly using these three powerful mental tools to our detriment. Mind Fitness gives us a rationale and structure in which to use these skills to our advantage so that we may gain control of our attitudes, behaviors, and life directions.

This mental focusing approach has three main components and is designed to enhance the quality of our personal and professional lives. It is a gentle but deliberate shift in perception—away from the habit of defeat and pessimism, toward learning the habits of fulfillment, productivity, satisfaction, joy, and internal balance.

Healing personal negativity also means:

- nurturing first and foremost a warmer, more confident and generous relationship with ourselves
- enhancing the depth and quality of our relationships with loved ones, friends, and coworkers
- enjoying a greater sense of direction and accomplishment in our work, community, and creative lives.
- living more optimally in areas of health, relationships, finances, and personal expressions of success.

For the purposes of this book, negativity is defined as "to see without love," meaning seeing the limitations and impossibilities first. Healing is defined as "to see with love," meaning to see the potential possibilities. The essence of Mind Fitness is the *deliberate choice* to do something regularly to enhance our minds' orientation and, therefore, our lives' direction.

Jerry Jampolsky, M.D., founder of the Center for Attitudinal Healing (located just outside of San Francisco, California), is a pioneer in this shift of thinking. He speaks about being a "love finder" rather than a "fault finder." This simple difference is what attitudinal psychology is all about.

Personal negativity patterns are ways of thinking we have *learned* and practiced; therefore, if we choose, we can transform them with new attitudes and behaviors that work *for* us rather than against us. This is the good news; hence the title, *The Up Side of Being Down.*

Let's look at attitudes for a moment. Attitudes are different from moods. Moods are like sunlight on a wall. They move around, change shapes frequently, bounce off various objects in different ways, and assume many different patterns in the course of a day. A stream of sunlight may exist right alongside the darkest shadow.

In contrast, attitudes are not as quickly changeable as moods. They are steadier, more like the sun itself. Our attitudes reflect our baseline emotions— "where we live" within ourselves. They are our basic orientation, determining whether we are happy, successful, optimistic people who feel whole within ourselves and view life as a challenge and opportunity, or people who let habitual negative thinking make life seem like an obstacle course.

We are in charge of what our attitudes will be. We may have developed habitual attitudes early in life, but they can always be changed to reflect what we want now. This flexibility—this ability to move from external to internal choices—lets us heal personal negativity and determine how we want to be in the world. We may have to overcome some early patterning and habits of thought, but repatterning and developing new, more loving and expansive habits of thinking is possible for everyone.

It boils down to this:

1.  Attitudes are the result of our personal, social, and cultural backgrounds and beliefs.
2.  Our attitudes influence both our moods and how we perceive and approach life.
3.  We have the power to choose what our basic attitudes will be.

We can learn new ways of thinking based on love, choice, responsibility, self-determination, and even happiness rather than on childhood helplessness, defensive anger, and fear.

When we start our own personal Mind Fitness training, we are making a *conscious choice* to take some control of our lives by putting ourselves into training that will result in our release from a condition that has been sapping our strength and energy for a long time. It is a choice for love, for growth, for health, for happiness, and for developing our creativity and richest potential in all fields of endeavor.

Sound like an ideal? It is the choice to actively focus and live a life designed around dynamic love and mental optimism.

# Chapter 2

## *MIND FITNESS*

Mind Fitness encourages the conscious use of our mind and spirit, on a regular basis, to heal negative thinking and replace it with more positive, creative, and enjoyable ways of relating to ourselves, to one another, and to our world. This is no add-on or extra; a regular mental health practice is integral to our ability to successfully function in the world.

As a framework for daily mental exercise and care, the practice of Mind Fitness leads to optimal health, creativity, and performance. Daily mental care does for the mind what physical fitness does for the body, and helps promote excellence by exercising mental attitudes with creative images and self-spoken directed words.

**"We become what we image"** is our operating premise. The regular practice of Mind Fitness calls on the mind's greatest untapped resource—the creative imagination— to form positive attitudes and then turn those attitudes into constructive action. Using the same core skills that peak performers use, we focus the mind, the will, and the imagination like a beam of light to help create the inner and outer realities we choose. By practicing our own program of Mind Fitness, we incorporate the conscious use of three powerful tools—relaxation, visualization, and affirmation—in our own personal program of self-development and growth.

### EXERCISE FOR THE MIND

We are just now beginning to know that, just as our bodies need proper nutrition and exercise in order to be healthy, our minds and souls also need to be fed, nurtured, and exercised with positive images and ideas in order to be healthy and peaceful. If we don't feed and exercise our minds and bodies properly, we experience deficiencies. For the body, the deficiency may be anemia or lack of muscle tone; for the mind, the deficiency may be chronic low energy, abusive anger, lack of self esteem, or other forms of negativity.

We can view our attitudes as muscles that can be toned, stretched, and made stronger. If we don't flex those attitudinal muscles, we're likely to stay mired in our old habits of fear and negativity. A few decades ago, we didn't know it was important to exercise our bodies. There was a time when we didn't even know we should brush our teeth! We're now making the same discoveries about our minds, and coming to understand that we humans *need a regular program of inner exercise and nourishment* to stay healthy, positive, and pointed in the directions in which we ideally want to go.

**We as individuals, and as a society as a whole, are realizing that "exercise" for the mind is as essential for our health and well-being as is exercise for the body. As we come to this realization, we are expanding our thinking about health.**

This is an expanding concept within the western world, one that this book aims to present in terms that are direct and meaningful in our high-stress culture—thus, the use of words "fitness" and "disease." We as a society have already accepted, intellectually, the need for regular physical fitness. I believe the next step in our growth is to accept the need for regular Mind Fitness.

Part of this daily-mental-care orientation is taking time out on a regular basis to care for our minds in much the same way that we take time to care for our bodies. Without "exercising" through relaxation combined with positive images and ideas, I believe that our minds are inclined to atrophy into negative or passive states, just as our muscles atrophy when they are not used. During our Mind Fitness time, we "pump images" in much the same way that some people "pump iron."

### TIME-OUT SESSIONS

Time out provides a time for disconnecting. It is a few minutes to relax our stressed-out, overworked minds and balance them with our bodies, bringing both to a place of receptivity. It is a time conducive to listening to our intuitive natures, understanding subtle points within the whole. A balanced mental state leads us in the right direction.

Just as saying a prayer helps us to imagine positive images, by saying affirming words, we *pump directive thoughts* specifically to move ourselves in the directions in which we want to move. We actually create a *personalized* program of daily mental focus and exercise. One month, the focus may be on a health need; another month, it may be a professional or personal direction, or a desired personality trait.

This quiet inner time is only part of the program. The Mind Fitness orientation involves a constant awareness that we are consciously growing and changing ourselves from within and altering our perceptions so that we live more creatively, contribute more to others, and learn to enjoy life more fully. We come to accept that we are evolving and need not be so afraid of changing our attitudes and actions as we learn more about ourselves and our world, and how to care for both.

We can do Mind Lifts—short mental exercises in the form

of constructive self-talk or reflective questions we ask ourselves—during the course of the day. As we drive across town, wait in line at the market, or prepare for a big exam, business meeting, or social date, we can take a few seconds or minutes to remind ourselves how we want to feel and what we want to accomplish. We can remind ourselves of our values and how we want to interact or perform.

Mind Fitness, like physical fitness, is a empowering program for our health and mental well-being. It stems from the decision to move forward in our own lives, choosing to change and grow, using regular mental care as a framework in which to focus on and accomplish our goals. We begin to take more responsibility for our thoughts, actions, and lives in general.

**Story:** Adele always told people, "I don't do sports." When people asked her to go skiing, play tennis, or even go along on bicycle trips, she always refused. As she began to examine this point of view about herself, she remembered something that had happened when she was in kindergarten. She and some other children were throwing a ball around. The teacher came up and laughed at her, calling her "uncoordinated." Rather than repeat that embarrassing moment, Adele just stopped participating in games and started saying, "I don't do sports. I am too uncoordinated."

Soon that point of view had become a reality as a personal constriction, a mental "dis-ability," holding her back from her full potential. She believed she was too uncoordinated to play sports, and she had never stopped to tell herself anything differently. When Adele started a self-development program, she thought about whether or not she wanted to continue that behavior, and decided that it was limiting her. She knew she might never become a great athlete, but she realized that there were probably some physical activities—bicycling and jogging, for instance—that she could do and would enjoy.

Adele's personal program of Mind Fitness included visualizing and affirming her ability to do those things and have fun with them. She first visualized herself doing different activities until she felt comfortable enough to try one.

She found, to her surprise, that the sport she decided to take up was tennis—not only for the sociability and the vigorous exercise, but because her visualizations had shown her that she was actually a competitive person. The thrill of winning was important to her and would hold her interest.

Armed with her newly focused direction and some courage, Adele signed up for a women's beginner class at the local tennis courts. She discovered that she loves the feel of the ball hitting her racket, and her coordination is just as good as her classmates'. In the past two years Adele has been regularly playing other women at her level—and, to her delight, she has become a pretty good tennis player.

### REGULAR MENTAL FOCUS

The practice of regular mental focusing teaches us how to use the mind as a bridge between our inner knowing—our intuition and true desires—and our capacity to act in the world. The "dream first, act second" model turns out to be an accurate learning model for human change.

We can use the powers of the focused mind, emotions, and imagination to shift, not just from negative to positive attitudes, but from others' ideas of what we should be and do to our *own* ideas of what we want to be and do. As a learning technology, Mind Fitness guides us to unlearn old habits and learn new ones, using specific thinking processes. We open up and sharpen our minds, enhancing the quality of our personal and professional lives.

Strong mental fitness creates better overall mental health supporting all areas of life: career, relationship, creativity, sports, learning, health, hobbies, finance, and so on. When we learn to think in focused ways, we see the results in our positive approach to each day, our ability to handle stress, our energy level, our self esteem, our sense of enjoyment and accomplishment in the quality of our relationships, and the generosity of spirit in which we hold ourselves and others.

Mind Fitness sessions help us learn to:

- **Break the cycle** of negative attitudes by recognizing and releasing those old habits, patterns, attitudes, and automatic reactions
- **Identify new goals** that are important to us—and move toward them
- **Turn new, positive habits** of thought into constructive actions that increase our well-being and satisfaction, so we are happier and can fulfill more of our potential
- **Make the transition** from fear and helplessness to active love and self-determination in our lives
- **Shift the focus** from psychological pain and emotional survival to love of self, generosity of spirit, and compassion for others
- **Build a solid base** of optimistic belief in ourselves from which to approach our lives and relationships with dynamic love.


*PROACTIVE REFLECTION*

The inner focusing practice  makes us aware of our thoughts, and lets us guide them to where we want to go. We identify personally destructive thinking, accept it, and replace it with powerful mental images of:

- how we want to feel and act
- what we want our lives to be, inside and out
- what we want to contribute and accomplish
- how to reach those goals

This approach of taking time out for personal proactive re-flection on our own behalf combines healing with empowerment, and lets us actively take charge of our lives. We consciously reflect on the kinds of perceptions and atti-tudes that we want to dominate our lives, and then translate those values into meaningful goals and actions. We actively use the mind as a bridge between our own inner knowing, our soul's journey, and our daily lives in the outer world. We take time out to think about who and what we are, to balance our emotions and set our energies in the direction in which we want to go. We don't solve all our problems immediately, but over time, as we approach them with growing conscious-ness and confidence.

The practice of inner quiet stimulates us to take charge of our lives in two ways: We clarify our desire to be a value-centered person interested in optimal health and well-being, and we take responsibility for whether or not we become that person.

Mind Fitness gives us a structure in which to heal—to connect with our inner strength and wisdom, to gently con-front our fears, to affirm our full potential. Using Mind Fit-ness principles, we identify our goals and visualize how to reach them, and confidently set out on that path.

### ADD-ON THINKING

The concept of daily mental care and exercise represents an evolution in the way we think about life and about ourselves. It is part of a natural progression toward higher levels of think-ing and interacting that enhance the way we live.

This evolution in thought is something I call Add-On Thinking. This term may bring to mind for some the "add-on" bus transfer in New York City, which allows passengers to add on to their ride at no extra cost. That's sort of what Add-On Thinking does—it allows us to expand our thinking, produce more change, and have better results in our lives, at no extra cost. It enables us to operate at levels we might have thought were beyond us.

In a simplified view, Add-On Thinking means calling on the brain's intuitive, creative, image-oriented functions to enhance the logical, analytical, language-oriented functions. We can think of it as having the two halves of the brain work together in ways that are integrated and synergistic, so that the whole is greater than the sum of its parts.

In our educational system, most of us have been taught to use only the "logical" brain—the "slice, dice, and shuffle" method of thinking. We learn and practice logical analysis, systematic reduction, and rational deduction with the result that each time, our thinking gets smaller and more precise. This is the scientific approach. We keep cutting up the hard facts in different ways and shuffling them into different combinations, but *few new ideas or perspectives enter the system*. The motto might be, "If it can't be proven, if it isn't logical and measurable, we don't want it."

The Mind Fitness process of thinking draws on these analytical skills—and adds on the creative, synthesizing skills, to include imaging and patterning. This is an integrative approach. It teaches "possibility thinking," using the imagination almost as a sixth sense to improve our health and performance in any activity. Taking the time to proactively reflect, we become more aware of who we really are—our shadows and our values—and how we interact with the rest of the world.

Both imaginative and analytical thinking are essential if we want to do and be our best. They are meant to *complement* one another, not *compete* with one another. The goal is to be grounded in the "real world" but also to foster creativity and personal development.

Because we are more accustomed to using the analytical function, we may have to put a bit more emphasis at first on learning about and working with the intuitive, imaginative abilities. These are skills that *can* be fostered by some attention on our part. Until now, we may have hesitated to call on this important resource in our pragmatic world, and some of us have reached the point that we have forgotten about our imaginative faculties and what they can do for us. This is correctable.

As we learn to recognize and use both powerful components of our minds, we become increasingly fulfilled and actualized as individuals. We become capable of bigger concepts and perceptions, aware of more subtleties and emerging patterns. We work closer to our potential and experience more of life because we enjoy greater insight. We see in different ways. We think of things we haven't thought of before. New ideas spring to mind. It's as if we've suddenly noticed a secret panel in a familiar room, even though it has been there all along.

Add-On Thinking acts like a synthesizing process. It takes us to a whole new level of thought, a distinct skill that nurtures creativity and innovation.

## GENEROSITY OF SPIRIT

As with physical fitness, people describe many benefits when they start incorporating a Mind Fitness orientation into their lives. Their relationships get better, they experience more satisfaction (and usually more success) in their work, they feel better physically and have more energy, they often play better tennis or golf, they generally get more involved in life and have more fun. Basically, people feel more in balance and assured of their direction.

The most important benefit many experience is a feeling that comes from deep within of kindness and generosity toward ourselves and others. There is a lessening of our fears as we get to know ourselves better. As we experience a daily time of relaxation and letting go, we are more willing to forgive and to accept. We are more emotionally in balance, more often. We expand our conscious awareness and increasingly understand that we all have both faults and magnificent qualities. This is borne out in our behaviors toward others, which may grow more compassionate and empathetic. We are less emotionally reactive. *As we quiet each day, we are less likely to condemn, and more likely to embrace others in a respectful and loving way.*

This enhanced ability to love, with its inherent generosity of spirit and compassion, extends not only to other people, as in our families and communities, but also to ourselves. The gentler we are with ourselves—the more we love ourselves—the more we are able to love others. And the more we love others, the more we are able to love ourselves. It becomes a dynamic upward spiral. The love and understanding we feel for ourselves and for others becomes an additional fuel that fires our success in work, in play, and in every area of life.

Love as an optimistic way of thinking is a learned behavior for those who want to learn. It means working through personal fears and opening up to others with some degree of trust. Even people who have difficulty relaxing and opening up can learn to enjoy more frequently that most pleasurable of human emotions, love.

**Story:** Richard is an insurance broker who came to one of our groups. When he shared that he had trouble opening up to people and felt overcome with shyness at times, no one doubted him for a minute. He sat in a posture that was completely closed—arms and legs crossed, chin on chest, eyes glued to the floor. At the same time, it was obvious that he desperately wanted more friendship and socializing in his life.

In the course of the meetings, as he practiced various Mind Fitness exercises, we saw Richard open up little by little, gradually feeling safe enough to extend himself to the other people in the group and also letting in their support and friendship. It didn't happen overnight, or even over the first month, but Richard made some important first steps in overcoming his shyness and people fears. At last report, he still surprises himself and others with his newfound ability to be present with them, to open up and share, to laugh and relax, and to basically love others—as well as himself.

Learning to love ourselves is at the core of Mind Fitness. Don't let the word "love" scare you off. It is very difficult to let ourselves be creative, healthy, and peaceful, leading what we so casually term "a happy life," if we don't love and accept ourselves. Positive supportive energy moves in a spiral cycle, touching us as it touches others. It is an attitude and a perceptual ground of being through which we view life in general. *Love means being willing to see the best and pardon the worst in ourselves and in others.* We enter into a radical trust as we open ourselves to each other, unconditionally believing that things eventually turn out for the best.

Self-love is an acquired or learned skill. Most of us are not brought up to love ourselves. Within much of the business, academic, and scientific worlds the word "love" itself is often thought of as inappropriate and too soft to be effective. We're brought up to *behave* ourselves, and not to be conceited or "full of ourselves."

The Mind Fitness philosophy gets around the harshness of this kind of upbringing by giving us a structure in which we are *supposed* to be kind and gentle with ourselves, in which listening to our own inner quiet is *necessary work*. It is important for us to do. It provides us with a rational excuse to be generous with ourselves.

A daily time of quiet and inner focusing helps us learn to approach the world not from the frantic helplessness, fear, and anger of infancy, but from the loving acceptance, self-determination, and generosity of a caring adult.

*HEALING*

Healing means recognizing and accepting our negative emotional and thinking patterns, and breaking these unwanted cycles as we focus on learning to see with expanded possibilities. The most difficult step is admitting to ourselves that we are more negative in attitude and perceptions than we want to be, and that we want to grow into a more open and optimistic person. In the pages ahead, we will learn how to help ourselves heal. To start us in that direction, it may be useful to look at some healthy attitudes, so we can begin to aim ourselves in that direction.

Here are some of the healthy attitudes and behaviors that help us break cycles of personal negativity:

- Our initial reactions to new people and things are welcoming and optimistic. We are open to the possibility that they will be a force for good in our lives.
- We value a sense of humor. We can laugh at ourselves and have fun easily.
- We are intimate and share ourselves fully without hiding behind cynicism, anger, depression, or criticism.
- We can admit to some negative feelings, knowing that they represent only a part of our experience—not all of it.
- We don't have to worry about whether or not we are happy.
- We do whatever feels right for us. We trust our intuition.
- We meet each day with self-confidence and some degree of favorable expectation, rather than with a gnawing dread.
- We have compassion for others. We can give freely without feeling that we are making a sacrifice. We want to support others in doing their best. We can admire others because we don't fear that we lose if they win.
- We feel good enough, worthy enough, in control enough to handle the tasks before us.

- We let ideas of who we are and what we want to do emerge from within ourselves, rather than having them dictated by external forces.
- We maintain a level of self-discipline that makes us feel good about ourselves. We are focused and have clear priorities.
- We feel a balance among the many aspects of our lives.

# Chapter 3

# WE BECOME WHAT WE IMAGE

Recent research shows that there are powerful connections between the mind and the body; between attitudes and actions; between what we think and what we do. It is becoming common knowledge that performance can be improved by first entering a relaxed state, and then visualizing and experiencing mentally the activity exactly as we would like to do it. The principles of mental rehearsal and visualization have been used extensively for peak performance in sports; now they are being put to use by professionals in business, education, medicine, and health.

More than ever before, we have come to appreciate that "thoughts are things." This ability to create self-fulfilling prophecies in our minds and to effect reality with mental images is how personal negativity thinking habits come into being—and how they are healed.

## THOUGHTS ARE THINGS

The idea that skills can be honed, attitudes enhanced, and performance improved by seeing the desired results in the mind's eye is not new. Visualization has long been used by optimal performers in all fields, and its effectiveness in sports has been obvious for some time.

What is new in the past twenty years is that the scientific

community has been testing and studying this phenomenon called the neurophysiology of learning. Scientists have come to agree that it is a powerful method of changing and improving both mental and physical conditions.

Increasingly, medical and educational research show that thoughts carry information that affects, and actually creates, overall physical health and peak performance. Dr. Willis Harmon, past president of the Institute of Noetic Sciences, writes "One of the most far-reaching of the findings related to consciousness has been dubbed the 'self-fulfilling prophecy.' More precisely, it is that our beliefs, conscious and unconscious, create the future in ways more subtle and more powerful than we ordinarily take into account."

In his introduction to Norman Cousins' *Anatomy of an Illness*, Rene Dubos writes, "Cousins repeatedly states that the mental attitudes of patients have a lot to do with the course of their disease and illustrates this theme with examples taken from clinical material. It is common knowledge, of course, that the mind influences the body and vice versa . . ."

At well respected institutions such as the Menninger Clinic, the Simonton Clinic, UCLA, Stanford University, and Harvard Medical School, doctors and researchers are showing that we can gain mastery over physiological functions through mental imagery, relaxation, meditation, visualization, and affirmation. These techniques have proven effective in normalizing heart rates, reducing stress, and decreasing pain in burn units, and may even be responsible for some unexplained remissions in cancer.

## PEAK PERFORMERS

People who want to be the best in their fields have not waited for research to validate methods that they knew worked. Some of the most accomplished people in the world use the principles of relaxation, visualization and meditation to achieve their optimal performance:

**Sports and Education:** Early pioneering leaders in the constructive use of focused thinking include such long-time great athletes as Masters golfer Jack Nicklaus, tennis champion Stan Smith, and seven-time American League Batting champion Rod Carew; and Olympic gold medalists such as skier Jean-Claude Killy, diver Greg Louganis, and swimmer Janet Evans. In sports, visualization is often referred to as mental rehearsal or sports psychology.

**Education:** Educators call these same techniques accelerated learning; they are applying skills that have been used for years in teaching. Mentally seeing and hearing is a skill that, once learned, can be applied to many areas of learning. This approach is now a part of the learning environment in many "can do" classrooms. In this course of study, students learn how to imagine their success in the classroom, on the playing field, and in their daily lives.

**Business and Medicine:** Corporations now acknowledge the value of creative intuition as well as logical analysis, and use visualization to plan and achieve individual and corporate goals. This interest is evidenced by the huge growth of corporate seminars aimed at developing peak performance and leadership skills in management staff. Increasingly, these seminars emphasize visual communication, including the use of imagination, mental rehearsal, and iconic symbols. It's all part of a corporate effort to increase creative problem-solving.

In medicine, the term "lifestyle diseases" refers to conditions that do not come from bacteria or viruses, but from continual life stresses that affect both body and mind. Pioneers in biofeedback and cardiology are demonstrating astounding relationships between the mind's thoughts and the body's cardiovascular and immune systems. Mental imagery has also proven helpful in dealing with some cancers, in childbirth, in reducing pain in burn clinics, and in promoting overall physical health. In the field of medicine, Mind Fitness techniques are usually called guided imagery, stress reduction, or wellness "techniques."

The optimal performance-enhancing skills common to all these fields are relaxation, visualization, and affirmation. Each program encourages optimal mental and physical performance through mental focusing—the conscious choice of, and concentration on, certain thoughts. *Proactive reflection encourages the individual to take the time and responsibility to determine for him or herself the desired outcome.* These principles can be applied to any endeavor. A jogger uses the same mental focusing skills to improve his running that a cancer patient uses to promote her body's well-being; an executive looking for a creative solution uses the same techniques as a student studying for an exam.

### *WORKING AGAINST OURSELVES*

Whether or not we are aware of it, we have been using these techniques all our lives. We have been imaging and visualizing each time we daydream, each time we roll something over in our minds. And many times we've imaged something, at least a part of it has manifested in our reality.

If there doesn't seem to be a pattern to this manifestation, it is because there probably hasn't been much pattern to our visualization. We are not taught to sit down, figure out what we want in life, and use visual imagery to achieve our goals. More importantly, we are not warned that if we sit around brooding, lost in negative thoughts or pondering resentments, we are actually creating negativity in our lives.

Given the lack of information we've received, combined with not knowing the amazing power of intuition and visualization, it's astonishing how well most of us have done! When we understand the power of visual imagery as an important, productive mind tool, we can begin to make our own choices and take an active role in what happens in our lives.

## WHAT WE CAN DO ABOUT IT NOW

What all this means is that we are in control of our own destinies. We begin by becoming aware of our personal learned patterns and triggers. What we have learned, we can unlearn. We have taught ourselves one thing; we can teach ourselves something else.

Our old negative viewpoints have been formed from feelings of helplessness, fear, and anger. We can use the same mental techniques to reshape those old viewpoints and shift our thinking so that our base of operation becomes love, self-determination, and growth. We can begin to *choose* the way we use these powerful tools of mental focusing. We are no longer helpless. It takes courage to accept our shadow, but once we do, we can teach ourselves to deal with the world as loving, accepting, creative adults.

Old patterns can be altered with thinking skills, and thinking skills can be learned. Thoughts create attitudes and actions, and we can learn to guide and amplify them. In order to change our lives, we need to discover which thoughts are making life the way it is, and consciously focus on changing those thoughts.

The ability to do this, through daily Mind Fitness exercising, allows our species to move beyond physical evolution to an evolution in thought, consciousness, and spirituality—an evolution in which we focus on literally recreating ourselves in the ways we want to be, an evolution that is only just beginning and has no known limits.

*MOVING FROM COPING TO CREATING*

I first encountered this idea of psychological and spiritual evolution in the works of Dr. Abraham Maslow. This evolution isn't physical; we don't need to grow a new kind of ear or eye in order to survive. What we need is a change in consciousness, a quantum leap in the way we perceive ourselves and our world. To make this leap, we must tap abilities and potentials that we have ignored or not developed until now. Mind Fitness, as an attitude-to-action approach to inner and outer peace, is designed to help us make such a leap in consciousness, personally and as a society.

Dr. Maslow's theory of personal development and human needs suggests that we move naturally from living life at the level of *coping*—just barely able to satisfy our physical and psychological needs—to living life at the level of *creating*, where we fulfill our potential and become self-actualized people.

When I first read in my undergraduate days Dr. Maslow's book, *Toward a Psychology of Being*, I felt as if I had been given a road map to how I wanted to develop and live my life. A light bulb went off in my head and I knew my path. Maslow described a human "hierarchy of needs," a progression from one level to the next. It goes like this:

**1. Physical Survival.** At this level, we are concerned about food, shelter, clothing, and physical safety. Most of our energy goes into physical survival. This level is characterized by fear and desperation, and our thinking tends to be survival-oriented. Before we can move on to the next level, we have to establish some degree of physical security, a base of safety in which our bodily survival is not threatened.

**2. Emotional Safety and Self-Worth.** The next level is psychological, and includes areas such as friendship, self-esteem, and winning respect from others. Maslow's research showed that when we are not feeling competent, or when we do not feel respected for who we are and what we do, our self-worth comes into doubt and we feel unsafe. This psychological deprivation leads to feelings of anger and hostility, and to harsh judgment of others. When we can't accept others, then we can't accept ourselves, which makes it even more difficult to accept others. It becomes a downward cycle. We are afraid not for our physical safety, but for our emotional safety and self-worth—still, we are living in fear. Before we can move on, we need to satisfy our needs to feel worthwhile and to be loved and respected by the people around us.

**3. Self-Actualization.** The first two levels involve physical and psychological security. This third level moves us into the spiritual realm, in which we begin to satisfy our needs to be self-expressive and creative. This is the area of optimal and peak performance. It might be in the arts, in sports, in higher learning. or in some other field, but this is the level at which we see extraordinary achievements and fully satisfied people. Maslow calls these people "self-actualized" or "fully human." They no longer live their lives out of a sense of deficiency or scarcity; rather, they feel an expansion, a sense of self-worth and confidence that makes more room in their lives for achievement and creativity. These self-actualized people live optimally and are capable of amazing achievements and success. Mind Fitness provides a framework in which to teach people how to become self-actualized and to live at this fully developed and optimal level.

Self-actualized people, according to Dr. Maslow, tend to have deep connections with others and to experience love not only for the people with whom they come in contact, but for all the human race. There is a spiritual aspect to their lives with a strong sense of the interconnectedness of all life, and a trust in their intuitive sense to guide them.

These are some of other ways Maslow's work has described self-actualized people:

- They enjoy life in nearly all of its moments and aspects, whereas other people have only limited moments of enjoyment.
- They are spontaneous, creative, open to new experiences, and relatively unafraid of the unknown.
- They have a feeling of dominion in their lives and demonstrate a healthy selfishness, which means they respect their own activities and guard their time accordingly.
- Their work and play tend to overlap and become equally absorbing and satisfying.
- Because of their strong self-knowledge and self-acceptance, and relative absence of fear, they are not hostile toward others.
- They are quick to love and be loved.

## OPTIMAL LIVING: DAILY MENTAL CARE

Mind Fitness brings together two powerful concepts:

1.  The concept of *daily mental care*—using the proven learning techniques of mental imagery and affirmations to influence our attitudes and our lives, and

2.  The concept that *we evolve and grow* by continually upgrading the quality of our lives—moving from physical survival, through emotional safety, to self-actualization with its powerful energies for love, creativity, and fulfillment.

The practice of Mind Fitness quickens our path toward self-actualization because it encourages us to listen inwardly and to *choose* exactly where we want to be on the hierarchy of needs. We can therefore focus on creating the lives we want. The techniques of relaxation, visualization, and affirmation take us beyond the physical and psychological realm into the spiritual realm, the realm of creativity and connection with the infinite. There we experience on a deeper level the meaning of unlimited capacity to be whatever we want to be, with no boundaries or limits.

We may choose to concentrate on peak performance in sports—improving our tennis game, running, or weight lifting. Our external goals may center on professional areas—self-improvement, a raise, a promotion, a change of careers, or being a better manager. We may want to concentrate on being excellent learners in order to master a new area of interest, or we may want to improve our health. We may want to concentrate on being better parents or spouses. *Optimizing one area of our lives always spills over into all the other areas.*

Living as loving and creative people is living life to the fullest. Mind Fitness thinking guides us to *choose* to optimize our lives, rather than just waiting around to see whether or not it happens.

### LOVE: THE BOTTOM LINE

Why go to all this trouble? Why not just wait and see what kind of cards life deals us?

Along with an evolutionary pull to continued personal development, I believe that what we all want more than anything else is to love. The desire to love and be loved is even more basic than the initial helplessness with which we enter the world. It is truly our home base.

**Expanding love and creativity are the focus of an actualizing life.**

Inner mental and spiritual focus is a way of life that guides us to move consciously *out* of our long-standing habits and our addictions of helplessness, fear, and anger, and *into* expressive lives built on love of self and others. This focus embodies the willingness to strive towards the possibilities, the optimistic, the positive—just as a plant reaches for the light.

This shift in thinking is the recognition that we, both personally and collectively, are moving—quickly or slowly—out of pessimism and into optimism, out of anger and into self-expression. Love is more than mere compassion; it is an expression of faith that we are all connected and that, on some level, we are all one striving for harmony and continued development. There is a sense of gratitude that dwells within our hearts and minds.

## CONSCIOUSLY DESIGN YOUR LIFE

An important part of practicing Mind Fitness is making the decision to consciously design your life around love. Dynamic love. Love that is constantly changing and growing as that mental attitude influences our lives. *Being a loving person is a skill to be cultivated and nurtured.* Because we're all human and subject to the pain, fear, and anger that become part of our makeup, we can't simply assume that love will just come to us without being called. We need to make known *our intention to love*—first and foremost to ourselves—and then we need to do something about it. As we become proactive for love, we start to focus on love as something we are consciously creating in our lives. Then the healing process begins.

One of the most well-publicized ways to start focusing on love is to write a Gratitude List. Each day, reflect back upon your experiences and write down five things for which you are grateful. These can be small moments, such as seeing a sunset, having correct change for the bus, or hugging your child in a quick moment of sweetness. As we consciously start to appreciate the small things of life, our fear and anger start to dissolve, controlling us less as they become more balanced within us emotionally. This first occurs on a personal level, then expands to our relationships, to our families, and on into the larger community.

Loving ourselves is at the very heart of strong mental health. In entering into this philosophy and orientation of caring for ourselves and reshaping our lives, we have given ourselves a gift—a gift of kindness and of self-determined power. We have begun to put our soul selves at the center of our own lives and sense our connection with something infinite—the spirit in all of us that allows us to go beyond what we thought we were.

# Chapter 4

## *THE BEGINNINGS*

We may have by now become aware that we have a negative slant on the world and have consciously decided that we want to work on a more positive and constructive life attitude. We may have decided to work on learning how to use the untapped power of our imaginative minds and spirits to become active in creating love, inner peace, creativity, accomplishment, and increased happiness into our lives. We may want to now be proactive by developing new mental habits that contribute more to the world and, at the same time, lead us to experience more joy, growth, pleasure, and satisfaction. When we begin to think like this, we've begun to opt for lives that are about self-determination and possibilities, rather than about limitations and barriers.

### *HOW PERSONAL NEGATIVITY MAY BEGIN*

The way negative mental and emotional patterns may get started is unique to each individual, but I believe there is a common thread that has to do with our early feelings of helplessness. Initially we experience harmony—the harmony of love and peace as we create and grow in the womb. All is tranquil and cared for in our world. Love and growth can be thought of as our home base.

Our birth brings many changes. The first thing that happens to us after birth is that we are deprived of a situation in which all our needs have been met. In the womb, we float effortlessly in an environment designed to do nothing but support us. We have a steady flow of nutrition; temperature and waste removal are never problems.

When we are born, despite the best of intentions, things start getting unpleasant very quickly. Suddenly, all of our needs are *not* met automatically, and there is nothing we can do about it. We are entirely helpless.

Helplessness is the first human experience (after birth) that we all share, and I think it becomes the foundation for most of our subsequent perceptions and understandings. It is the initial fact of life for everyone. Our original place of love and peace has been shattered. Now we are totally dependent, unable to care for ourselves, and we must rely on others for food, protection, cleanliness, and affection.

Helplessness quickly prompts feelings of fear. We feel threatened and vulnerable. We *are* vulnerable. If we are left on our alone, the chances are good that we won't survive. All young children share the fear of being abandoned—and with good reason. Professionals tell us that one of the worst things that we can do to a toddler is to pretend we're going to leave him if he doesn't hurry. It reinforces this deep fear of being unable to care for himself in the world and being left behind by the people who *do* take care of him.

So we can't take care of ourselves, and the people who are supposed to take care of us don't always do a perfect job. As babies we were fed foods we didn't like, we didn't get changed as often as we wanted, we had our bottoms wiped in ways that were uncomfortable and may have hurt, we were made to do things we didn't want to do, and we were not allowed to do things we wanted to do. We may have been tossed in the air when we were scared, or tickled past the point of fun, or played with while experiencing fear and frustration.

Many were outrightly abused physically and/or psychologically, intentionally or unintentionally. Only now are we, as a society, beginning to realize the psychological damage of many of the child-rearing practices we found acceptable in the past. Many things are coming out of the closet and seen as part of the taproot of negativity. As adults, many are seeking out support groups to learn how to move past their fears and angers to live more trusting and peaceful lives.

We all have experienced the fears and frustrations of not being in charge of our own lives, and many have been upset with the people who had control over them. It may have looked different for each of us, but by the time we were about five years old, we all have experienced *original anger.* Original anger is the anger we have inside as a result of early life experiences. After birth we experience a degree of helplessness that often leads to fear and then to an insidious anger. Once we identify and accept our anger and negative reactions, we want to learn how to experience our home base of love.

## *THE ATTITUDE GROWS*

As we grew, we dwelled on these early fearful feelings, reacted to them, and all too often let them set the tone for our mental fantasy play. Thus, the basic attitudinal backdrop to our lives was formed. This is especially true if we suffered from physical or psychological abuse and other extreme forms of negativity.

Fantasy is an important part of any child's play. This childhood mind-play is a powerful tool that can be used to our detriment or to our advantage. The versions of mind-play are endless, and personalized to fit each individual life. When we were young, we didn't have much wisdom in handling this potential tool and we got little instruction. As a result, many of us used our mind-play in ways that later turned out to be limiting and self-destructive. We did not realize that our fantasy play could have such a potent effect on our lives, or that it could crystallize into a lifelong habit of thinking.

Most of us can remember how, as teens, we retreated to our rooms and continued a somewhat more sophisticated version of this imaging and fantasy play. We daydreamed for hours, fueled by all the emotions that came from not experiencing our home base of love: fear, anger, sadness, frustration. We saw ourselves as, victims, even as martyrs. We developed coping mechanisms: resistance, toughness, whining, "getting even" in petty ways—whatever we thought could help us make it through those difficult years.

If we felt accepted and in control of our lives, we probably used our imaginations more constructively and fantasized about being heroic, clever, successful, or artistic, or about incredible athletic feats. The many hours we spent in mental play created a mental self-portrait and belief system. This set the tone for our attitudes as adults. During those years, we started developing the positive and negative filters through which we now view life. We were actually teaching ourselves a *learned* response to the people and events around us.

I believe that our emotion-packed daydreams in early childhood and through our teen years set an attitudinal tone that affects everything we do and see as adults. If we concentrated on blaming others for our feelings of helplessness and anger—with feelings of "I can't" or "They're picking on me" or "Poor me" or "I always get the short end"—then we taught ourselves a predominant perception of the world: one filled with feelings of fear, bitterness, impatience, defeatism, and despair. Our governing theme became "I never win, life is hard, and I am not in control." In contrast, if we spent our time daydreaming constructively about our abilities, we were more likely to emerge as adults who approach life with a sense of satisfaction, fulfillment, and self-confidence.

This is the way that predominantly negative thinking patterns begin, and how they grow during adolescence as we literally teach ourselves to approach life with varying degrees of positive or negative thinking—usually without any idea whatsoever of what we are doing. As adults, these clusters of attitudes and behaviors are so much a part of us that we hardly know they are there. They form our basic thinking mode, and we cannot change it until we have recognized the pattern and the source.

So how do we recognize personal negativity in ourselves? What is it, exactly, that hurts? How can we refocus our perceptions?

### CUSTOM-MADE

Everyone experiences negativity differently. Can you recognize any of these feelings?

- Insatiability: a sense that there is never enough (love, money, food, sunshine, cleanliness, beauty, and so on), a feeling of never being satisfied; "I want more!" or " The grass is always greener on the other side of the fence."
- Endless complaining and whining: a feeling of being defeated and victimized by the world: "They didn't let me," or "They did it to me."
- Anger, irritation, a habit of springing into self-righteous judgments without warning or provocation: "You idiot! You did it all wrong. I could have done it better."
- Dark feelings of apathy or depression: "What's the use? Nothing will work anyway."
- Never being able to do or be enough: "I just wanted to . . ."
- Feeling pressured and overwhelmed: "I will never be able to do all of this," or "I am the only one who works this hard."
- Haunting fears and phobias that keep life from being expansive and fulfilling: "I don't know why, but I just can't do it. I am scared."

Negativity is an overriding feeling of resistance to every task and opportunity. Nothing seems to be easy—or if it is, it is made more difficult by being plagued with doubts, and indecision, and unfavorable judgments. Commonly, the responsibility for feelings and life is placed on the *external*, with a negative, self-limiting twist. These feelings are self-imposed and subjective and often are not in sync with worldly success.

This syndrome of shadow emotions and behaviors manifests itself in as many ways as there are individuals who experience it, but most often in the form of beliefs and feelings that life is unfair—with a predominant reaction of helplessness, insecurity, defeatism, fear, and anger. Often these feelings consume us without our conscious awareness.

None of us will ever be perfect, with a *constantly* "up" slant on life. (Even the most devoted monks have their down days.) We cannot expect to "correct" *every* attitude that keeps life from being as full or happy as it might be. But in order to change any of these attitudes, it's essential to identify them. Then we can plan active strategies for replacing the old attitudes with new ones, to heal old hurts and begin living more positively and fully.

### PROTECTION AND SURVIVAL

We didn't come into the world with automatic negative reactions. We learned these attitudes and behaviors as responses to our early environments, as means of surviving what we thought we could not survive in any other way.

For the most part, we learned these behaviors *unconsciously*. We simply did what we thought we needed to do at the moment in order to successfully protect ourselves, and then we adopted those behaviors as a way of living life—again, without much thought. Twenty, forty, or sixty years later, we find ourselves using those same behaviors—whether or not they're relevant to anything in our lives now. They may have been effective, even necessary, back then. However, today, if we examine them, we can see that they have simply become long-standing *habits* that we use mostly in response to varying degrees of stress. They do not lead us toward a happier, more fulfilled life—in fact, they stand in our way.

When Stan examined his pattern of coming down with a cold or the flu whenever his wife had to go out of town on business, he realized that when he was young, he never felt that his mother paid enough attention to him except when he was sick. He had unconsciously adopted the habit of getting sick whenever he felt threatened by a lack of attention—and he had kept the pattern long after it had stopped working. Sometimes we consciously adopt certain behaviors as a conceived plan of action—a way to handle a situation that feels out of control, or to blunt physical or emotional pain. The problem is, this strategy stifles our happiness just as effectively as it stifles the pain.

**Story:** In a seminar, Ann related that she had been raised in poverty, and been determined to make a success of her life. She was a hard worker, and by the time she was twenty-five had put together the money and backers to buy a small boutique in Chicago. The belief she had adopted in order to pull herself up by her bootstraps was that she always had to be working hard, solving problems, making improvements, and going at a project full steam ahead, or everything would crash and burn. Relaxing wasn't something she could even consider. It simply wasn't possible.

This is how she approached the new boutique. She worked around the clock, and sure enough, it was a huge success. Ann got what she wanted.

The problem arose when Ann discovered that it wasn't so easy to let go of this "full steam ahead" attitude. She harbored the fear that, if she ever let up, all her success would vanish overnight and she would feel terrible about herself. She had become a perfectionist. She couldn't rest until everything at home and at work was in perfect order. She was always pushing herself to do more, to find something that hadn't been done.

Ann began to realize that not only was *she* not having any fun with her life, but she didn't have many friends left. Her woman friends stopped calling her because she never came along with them. Men found her exhausting and difficult to please. She began to see that she was out of balance with herself.

The very characteristic that had brought her success had become a part of her negative stress pattern. She had adopted the need to work and to achieve in order to get control of her life, but now that same need was controlling *her*.

This story illustrates three points:

1. We need to reach a certain level of awareness to even begin to identify areas of our life that are out of balance. That in itself shows good growth.

2. We want to be gentle and forgiving with ourselves as we start to identify the patterns of negativity within us. We adopted these attitudes and behaviors for good reasons; in many cases, we needed them to survive. The problem is, we forgot to update ourselves and let go of these habits when they were no longer useful to us. It's to our credit that we are doing that now.

3. The simple awareness of identifying the area of negativity and targeting it for healing actually begins the process. Once we know what we want to focus on, some of the subtle work actually begins without our having to do much on the conscious level. Of course, there are many things we can and want to do beyond that initial identification, but we also need to give ourselves credit for having the courage to face things that are very uncomfortable.

## USE NEGATIVITY AS A TEACHER

The Chinese teach that all crisis leads to opportunity. We can use our personal forms of negativity as a blessing in disguise. This is the Up Side of Being Down. It teaches us to know ourselves better, to transform negative into positive, and to tap mental powers that we might never have used. It teaches us the art of making mistakes and correcting them. It shows us how to use symptoms as springboards for growth, and to benefit from what at first appear to be problems.

We've all heard the old expression, "It's not what you see that can hurt you; it's what you *can't* see." Those who haven't taken the time and energy to look at the negative, self-defeating aspects of their personalities often find that they are undermined by those unconscious beliefs. We all have those parts of ourselves. Only when we look straight at them, with honesty and love, can we begin the process of moving forward on our path of fulfillment—for ourselves, and for the contributions we can make to the world at large. When we have the courage to look at our darker side, we can begin to manage and then to heal it. Those negative feelings don't sneak up on us as often, and we're able to recognize and refocus them when they do. It's trite but true to say that it is only when we have examined our personal dark side that we can really know our light.

As long as we deny the negativity within us, it has power over our lives. When we put all our energy into resisting the negativity or pretending it's not there, it has control of us. That is where most of us have been. We cannot deal with what we refuse to see, and so it continues to fester beneath the surface, pulling our strings, until we bring it into the light and look at it directly. This is the time when a good therapist or personal development support group can be so meaningful to our growth. Though personal development is a subjective self-examination process, we often need others to mirror what they see in us. We cannot see everything about ourselves, by ourselves; it is too much a part of us.

**Story:** Beth was an overachiever who could never acknowledge her feelings of unworthiness. She had these feelings so well hidden behind the mask of her professional accomplishments that even *she* wasn't aware of them. Beth was an extraordinarily successful attorney—she had been appointed a judge before she turned 35—but her personal life suffered. She kept herself aloof from friends and had trouble making connections with men because, beneath all the success, she felt unlovable and unworthy.

She became so distressed with her failure on the personal side that she came to a workshop, where she got in touch with those subtle feelings of personal unworthiness. Once she could see what the problem was, she was off and running to fix it. She devoted her considerable energy to putting together a self-directed Mind Fitness program that emphasized feeling lovable and deserving. She also decided to seek counseling expertise to delve deeper into her past and discover how it was affecting her today.

Beth's initial experience of negativity actually turned out to be a gift. She uncovered a part of herself that was sabotaging her, and that might have stayed hidden if she hadn't felt the pain and done something about it. In the process, she also learned some strategies for continued personal development and some tools she could use to deal with self-defeating attitudes and feelings in the future.

The ability to use negativity as a teacher lets us turn these self-sabotaging experiences into positive ones. Negativity shows us how we are falling short of our higher aspirations—and where we need to work.

# Chapter 5

## *SYMPTOMS AND PAYOFFS*

The habits of limiting and negative thinking can be elusive. They can hide behind symptoms of other conditions, or they can seem to disappear entirely into the fabric of our lives. Sometimes they are so pervasive that they can hardly be seen at all—we "can't see the forest for the trees." Everything we perceive is tinted, but we can't actually see these "dis-eases" of negativity. There are no rashes, bumps, or swellings in attitudinal disorders.

This list of symptoms may help pinpoint where you stand. This is intended only as a guideline. Obviously, no one will have every behavior or attitude on the list. On the other hand, having a few symptoms does not mean that your life has been completely taken over by negativity. We are not bad people but we do want to have the courage now to identify, accept, and forgive our own personally limiting patterns. Then we can move ahead to healing ourselves of unwanted reaction patterns.

You may recognize characteristics on this list that have also been used to describe other newly named behavior syndromes. These "dysfunctions" are related to each other, with many of the identifying behaviors overlapping. Thus, it's useful to speak in terms of a *generalized negativity*—this allows people the means to relearn and heal *any* set of beliefs, thoughts, or attitudes that are limiting their lives. They don't have to place the blame on themselves or anyone else, or decide whether they were abused, addicted, children of alcoholics, a woman who loves too much, or whatever the form may be. They can simply go ahead and begin to identify their limiting attitudes and thinking patterns, replacing those old worn-out perceptions and beliefs with more empowering and expanding thinking.

Any cluster of attitudes or behaviors that diminish our aliveness and enjoyment of life is part of this syndrome. Those that follow are the ones that people mention most often.

### *"THAT'S IMPOSSIBLE"– THE HABIT OF DEFEATISM*

Those who are ruled by this habit approach most things as if they are impossible. They place the burden for proving that it *might* be possible on someone else. The first reaction to new opportunities or situations is usually, "I couldn't do that." This self-defeating attitude of "I can't" or "I shouldn't" makes everything feel "too hard."

Judy always saw herself as inadequate and incapable of doing "anything of importance." She held conversations with herself that confirmed her worthlessness and incompetence. Right out loud, she said things like "There, I've done it wrong again. I'm always so stupid . . . Look how I did that . . . I knew I wouldn't do it right."

Needless to say, this defeatist chatter became a self-fulfilling prophecy. It's very difficult to do a good job when we sabotage everything we attempt. Even normal mistakes threw Judy into a tailspin and confirmed her already low opinion of herself.

Judy's recovery from the habit of defeatism began with identifying and accepting her attitude. Once she understood that she had a habitual way of perceiving herself in the world, and that this perception almost always worked to her detriment, she could begin to do something about it.

Judy began to shift her focus to identifying and articulating what she *did* do well, and to create positive mental images and affirmations around her successes. She learned to acknowledge even the smallest accomplishment, and to replace her sweeping, generalized perceptions of stupidity with more narrowly defined areas in which she experienced difficulty. Her inner mind work focused on recalling all the situations each day in which she had done an activity "right." This meant recalling such taken-for-granted tasks as doing a good job at work, balancing her checkbook, making a dinner for guests, enjoying herself while she was out exercise-walking, stopping by to see her friend who was not feeling well, and so on. From this, she began to develop a more honest picture of her abilities and talents. She began learning how to assert her own worth, which touched virtually every area of her life.

Sometimes this habit of defeatist self-chatter can make even particularly good situations feel bad. Betty constantly berated herself for being "scattered." She was always coming up with new ideas for social actions and improvements that she could make in her community. One month she would work on better ambulance service; the next month she'd focus her attention on a zoning crisis, a child-care facility, or a problem in the school system. She berated herself because she didn't stay long with any one cause and was constantly moving around, never accomplishing anything that really changed the world.

Betty wanted to perceive herself in a way that would be more integrated and fulfilling. The key for her was to find the common thread running through all of her work.

As she pictured herself in her mind's eye, she began to see a circle with herself in the middle. All around her, on the circumference of the circle, were the various causes with which she was involved. She began to see that she was an important catalyst for all these causes and that, in fact, her job was to keep moving and catalyzing change. The self-definition that bridged all of her activities and integrated her work was "catalyst for social good."

Instead of thinking about how the ambulance people, or the school people, or the child care people would perceive her (as one who was only partly involved), she began to concentrate on how she perceived *herself*. Putting herself at the center of the circle and giving herself permission to adopt the self-definition of "catalyst for social good" integrated the various activities in her life and actually let her take on more of them without guilt or self-chatter.

The part of the story I love is that Betty went on to become mayor of her suburban town and is now *really* making changes!

### *"I'M HAVING A CONNIPTION FIT" – ANGER or DEPRESSION*

These are big symptoms, known to many people. Anger and depression both stem from fear. Anger results when the emotions are turned outward toward others; depression often results when they are turned inward against ourselves. If we are in the habit of blaming others, we are more likely to be angry. If we are in the habit of feeling guilty or unworthy, we are more likely to be depressed.

I'm not suggesting that we should never feel angry or depressed. These are normal human emotions, and can actually spur us on to greater accomplishment and growth if we are able to express them and use them productively. What I'm talking about here is *chronic* anger or depression—the kind that swoops down, seemingly from nowhere, and stays for long periods of time. This is the kind of anger or depression that we don't feel that we can do anything about and that is inclined to overwhelm us.

Some of the situations that prompt anger or depression are:

- feeling powerless, out of control, or unable to cope
- feeling unable to get our own way
- hearing people say things we don't like or want to hear
- thinking that our rights have been violated by others, or that someone has taken advantage of us
- feeling unappreciated or unacknowledged
- having an experience that reminds us of early childhood events in which we felt particularly powerless, angry, or fearful

It's important to identify and deal with our anger and/or depression for three reasons:

1.  Sometimes anger or depression that is unrecognized or suppressed takes the form of a generalized hostility. Everything has a negative twist. Whether we lash out or maintain a stony silence, the message is "Stay away from me." Obviously, this inhibits love and growth, and puts a wall around us that keeps out much of life.
2.  When anger is denied or allowed to fester unattended, it can burst forth unexpectedly and violently, harming ourselves or others.
3.  Research shows that people who are chronically angry or depressed tend to develop physical ailments and diseases. Cancer is the disease mentioned most often. Cancer involves a rampant overproduction of attacking cells, much as an angry individual randomly attacks people he knows. Anger is indeed physically toxic.

We think of depression as sadness, but it is more often simply a *depressing*, or shutting down, of all our systems—physical, mental, emotional, and spiritual—almost as if we were in hibernation or walking through molasses. We can feel heavy and overwhelmed by life to the point that we just want to curl up into a ball and hide.

Physical and mental pain can be deeply connected. Our bodies become storehouses for the negativity generated by our thoughts and attitudes. Sooner or later, this affects our physical health, which in turn affects our psychological health. It becomes a vicious cycle. Chronic *fears* about our health can produce the same result.

We all know angry, negative people who wear the marks of these attitudes on their faces in the form of deep frown lines and downturned mouths. We have seen pessimistic people who feel victimized and burdened walking around with stooped backs, looking as if they were physically weighed down, burdened, overloaded. On the other hand, we all know people who are joyful and optimistic, and whose bodies reflect that openness, flexibility, and adaptability. They move with ease and grace, and their smiles seem to reflect an inner peace and strength.

Anger and depression are two of the most challenging aspects of personal negativity, because they feel so powerful and out of control. The Mind Fitness philosophy emphasizes learning to listen to our intuitive selves clearly and honestly, and trusting in the process. By encouraging such self-determination in our focus, we learn to let go of the helpless feelings that often prompt anger.

### *"MELANCHOLY, CRY BABY" – SADNESS*

This too is a normal human emotion that only becomes problematic when it becomes extreme, pervasive, or chronic.

If a love one has just died, we expect to feel sad—for quite a while. In the wake of a personal trauma like losing a job or a forced move to a different part of the country, we have a right to grieve. Many experts now realize that we need to grieve whenever there is a major change in our lives. We grieve for the old, even when the new thing is something positive—the birth of a baby, promotion to a new job, or marriage to a wonderful new spouse.

We need to allow ourselves these kinds of sadness and mourning, but we don't want to let sadness or melancholy become the base from which we operate—or an excuse never to try anything new or challenge ourselves, never to go out of the house or to become emotionally involved. In other words, when the sadness and self-pity keep us from taking responsibility for our own lives and happiness, we may have crossed the line into just plain feeling sorry for ourselves.

When Richard lost his middle-management job at a computer company, it was a tremendous shock to him and his family. His wife Sally had a good job, but the two kids were in private schools and the family could just barely scrape by on her salary. Richard decided to take a few weeks off before starting to look for a new job, just to get his feet on the ground emotionally and take what he considered to be a well-earned vacation.

He had been an overachiever all his life, and the loss of this job was a sharp blow to his ego. Richard's emotional tailspin took the form, not of anger, regret, or guilt, but of a slow-burning, rather bitter sadness. He lay around the house, at first reading, then doing practically nothing. Soon he hardly had the energy to get out of bed in the morning unless Sally prodded him before she left for work. Nothing seemed to matter to him. The sadness had become a wall that kept him protected from everything else in life.

Finally Sally's patience and the family finances reached the point of crisis, and Richard sought help. He realized that the main thing his sadness kept him from feeling was *failure*. That was the one thing he had never wanted to experience, and here it was, right in his face. In fact, he hadn't failed—his firing had stemmed from cutbacks, not poor performance—but "failure" was the name Richard attached to losing one's job.

Richard also realized that if he didn't take responsibility

for having lost that job, he could never move forward and get a new one. Mind Fitness techniques enabled Richard to:

- RELAX, physically and mentally and get to a place where he was in truth with himself.
- VISUALIZE what he wanted, and ways to get there
- AFFIRM in words what was positive and working in his life right now and what skills he had to offer

Through this process, he began to accept his strengths and weaknesses as part of being human and began to regain his balance in life. Within a month, he had found a job he liked and he began to feel stronger within himself.

### *"THE TOUGH ONE" – CRITICISM, CYNICISM, AND RIGHTEOUSNESS*

The clever person often manifests insecurities by striving to appear better than anyone else. The hallmarks of this symptom are clever, sarcastic, or critical remarks that put down or make fun of everything and everyone.

People who suffer from this form of negativity find it hard to resist taking potshots at others—and sometimes at themselves. They adopt a "class clown" behavior rather than admit their underlying lack of self-esteem. By making cynical jokes and putting things down, they develop an identity that gets them the attention they crave . . . but it's not the kind of attention they really want. Often, they have an unconscious belief that if others get ahead, they will be left behind—that if others win, they will lose. They want to seem superior so that they won't lose their edge, and this often takes the form of being highly critical.

I was once called into a corporate setting to work with a man who management valued highly. He did excellent work, but was so sarcastic that his coworkers did not want him on their team. This man was brilliant at seeing people's weakest points and then letting them have it with some clever, demeaning remark. His intelligence was obviously high, but his generosity of spirit was lacking and he was hurtful to others. He told me he "needed to be tough or others would get to him." It's very difficult for people with that mind-set to be generous or forgiving. He didn't want to be considered "soft" or "stupid."

People who rely on this pattern of criticism, cynicism, and righteousness find it difficult to break, for two reasons:

- They are often successful, bright, and outgoing. Their identity is tied up in their verbal brightness. They usually think their intelligence is responsible for whatever social success they have achieved, and they are afraid that they will lose their edge if they stop publicly snipping and demeaning others with witty or cutting remarks.

- They realize that other people enjoy their Don Rickles-type performance, and don't want the practitioners to give up their "routines" because they are so entertaining. One seminar participant came back later and told me, "My friends all say 'I liked you better when you were cutting, sarcastic, and cynical!'"

**Tough cookie:** Another aspect of this pattern is the emotionally closed, "tough cookie" veneer. Alice told us that she was an oldest child in her family, and when she was growing up, she was responsible for baby-sitting for the three younger children. She felt as if she was always taking care of everybody's needs. Around age sixteen she rebelled. Her formerly sweet and docile nature took on a bitter, sarcastic edge that bordered on being nasty. She began being purposely mean to the younger kids, so her mother was afraid to leave them with her. It worked. Since she was no longer trusted, she didn't have to assume responsibility for anyone's care.

Her hostility got Alice out of being the family's "little

mother," but as she turned thirty, she realized that other people were just as put off by the chip on her shoulder as her family had been. She had difficulty establishing friendships, was seldom involved in relationships, and was inclined to have trouble with coworkers. The behavior that had worked so well when she was a teen was no longer working at all, but Alice had forgotten to "turn it off."

As she became aware of what had happened, she was gradually able to let the "tough cookie" act go and began to rebuild her gentler, more caring nature.

### *"SEEING THROUGH GRAY-COLORED GLASSES" – PESSIMISM*

This is the attitude that things probably *won't* turn out for the best—or if they do, it's going to be very, very painful. Pessimism can become a filter through which we see everything in life, an attitude of "guilty until proven innocent" rather than "innocent until proven guilty." Everything is a drag. We see the glass half empty, instead of half full, and are quicker to see the down side than the up side.

Sometimes we do this to protect ourselves from disappointment. If our expectations are extremely low, they are more likely to be met. If we don't really think the relationship is going to work out, or that we're going to get the raise or the promotion, then we won't be as disappointed or hurt when those things don't happen.

Of course, we set up a series of self-fulfilling prophecies. Pessimism doesn't usually foster personal or professional success, and when we don't succeed, we have even more reason to be pessimistic next time.

Ralph found himself in this position with women. "The women I find attractive are never interested in me," he said. With this attitude, he approached every date defensively, expecting either to be uninterested in the woman, or to be rejected. His lack of confidence and his "beaten puppy" demeanor did nothing to enhance his effect on women. He was a living example of the old Groucho Marx line, "I wouldn't want to belong to any club that would have me as a member."

Ralph's habit of pessimism caught him in a downward spiral. When he began to recognize his fears of rejection, he began to visualize other ways of handling various situations. Using his imagination skills, he "rehearsed" what it would mean to be willing to approach each relationship as if it actually might work. He experienced greater peace of mind and his social life took a turn for the better.

### "THE REGULATOR" – A HIGH NEED FOR CONTROL

This high need for control can take many forms: perfectionism at work; immaculate standards, from personal hygiene to housekeeping; safe relationships; rigid viewpoints; fears of change; compulsive behaviors and phobias; any set of attitudes that limit the boundaries of our own or others' speech or actions.

Some people in seminars describe this desperate need for control as a feeling of actually being *out* of control, helpless, and "just barely hanging on." We're afraid that if we ever stopped holding everything up, it will all crash in around our shoulders; that if we don't nail everything down, it will blow away; that, left to its own devices, the world will go awry.

Renee noticed her unusually high need for control when an old college friend visited from out of town. Renee was forty-two and had lived alone since her divorce at age thirty-five. Everything in her condo had an established place, just as everything on her desk at work was set up just so.

Trouble began almost as soon as Renee's friend Evelyn arrived in Seattle for a long weekend. Not only did Evelyn put things back in the wrong place after doing the dishes, she left splashes around the bathroom sink and was put out when Renee wouldn't let her borrow her car.

After Evelyn left, Renee started to see herself through her old friend's eyes and realized that she had become pretty compulsive. She was the only person she knew, for instance, who never let other people borrow her car.

As she spent some time in quiet proactive reflection, Renee realized that a great deal of her need for control came from feeling *out of control* in her life. She wanted to be in a relationship, and didn't seem to be able to make that happen. She wanted to buy a house, but never seemed to have enough for a down payment.

Just recognizing the problem took a lot of the pressure off, and Renee could start working on the real issues. Self-doubt is usually a part of that out-of-control feeling. When we stop trusting that we can handle the situation and begin to doubt ourselves, we open the door to fearful thoughts that can ambush us when we least expect it. We become tentative; we close ourselves off from positive opportunities because we're afraid they won't work out.

Just as self-doubts can bring about an attack of negativity, an infusion of self-confidence can transform it. In the second part of this book, we will discuss how to turn self-doubt into confidence through taking a few minutes daily for inner focusing.

### *"MISMATCHED" – INTERNAL AND EXTERNAL*

### *REALITIES DON'T MATCH*

We say we're "just fine," but we know we're not. We say nothing is wrong, but in fact, nothing seems right. We look fine on the outside, but feel tormented on the inside. We are not telling the truth. We don't want to bother people; we want things to look "just fine." We are playing a game of social illusion.

There are variations: We may feel fine at home, but our world falls apart when we go to work. Or conversely, we may feel okay at work, and be unhappy and overwhelmed at home. We may even behave quite differently in the two places.

We get our ideas of who we should be and what we should be doing from other people, rather than letting who we really are and what we really want to be doing emerge from within. Because we get our clues about how we should be from the external, our minds tell us one thing and our emotions experience quite another. We are mismatched, and out of sorts.

### "SHIFTY" – RESTLESSNESS AND DIFFICULTY FOCUSING

This feeling that there is no center to our activities can happen at work, at home, or both. We feel scattered, rushed, overloaded, and hopeless about ever getting it all done. We keep changing directions, and have trouble finishing tasks. We often set our goals too high, so nothing seems attainable and we almost don't feel like trying. It's high stress and anxiety.

"I was lucky just to make it through the day, let alone accomplish anything or have any fun," says Maggie, who manages a household and works part-time for an accountancy firm. "It was a struggle to stay centered, because I wasn't putting myself in the middle of this fast-spinning wheel. I was overwhelmed and felt pulled in a million directions. I had no idea where *I* wanted to go."

Maggie still does many of the same things and has the same schedule, but she has learned how to prioritize her activities, allowing her to go through each day with more of a sense of control, balance, and, yes, even some feelings of completion, rather than scattered frustration.

### *"MOAN AND GROAN" – DISSATISFACTION*

Satisfaction has less to do with the activities we perform than with how we feel about ourselves when we do them. I've spoken with corporate executives, doctors, therapists, and others who have accomplished a great deal in the world's eyes and have a high impact on other people's lives, yet really don't feel much satisfaction in their work. And I've spoken with other people whose contributions are less public, and who experience great satisfaction in doing things that are considered mundane, such as painting walls, filing, cutting grass, even ironing.

Of course, there are highly successful people who love their work, and people who chafe in mundane jobs. My point is that satisfaction comes more from within than from the people or circumstances outside ourselves.

Here's my satisfaction rule of thumb: If I like doing something about four days out of five, I am in good shape. We all have bad days, but when we experience chronic disappointment and dissatisfaction—when we are dissatisfied more than we are satisfied—something is wrong. Chances are we have stumbled into one of the forms of negative thinking.

### *"IT AIN'T MY FAULT" – FEELING VICTIMIZED*

We all know people who go through life as "professional victims." Nothing ever really works for them—love, money, job, family, you name it—and it's always someone else's fault. If there is no specific person on whom to pin the blame, they'll blame "fate," or "the times," or "society."

In its exaggerated form, this symptom means feeling that "I was just lying there, and the train came by and hit me"—feeling that someone or something is out to get us, and the best we can do is to react and dodge the next bullet.

It's a very painful way to go through life, and doesn't lead to much happiness or growth. There *are* ways to deal with this feeling and replace it with attitudes that embrace life and its challenges.

### "*I'M NOT OKAY AND NEITHER ARE YOU*" – *GUILT*

When we notice that guilt has become the coin of our realm— the thing that we use to pay people and that we demand from them in return—it's time to stop and see what's really going on.

When we feel guilty, or when we want the people around us to feel guilty, it's a clue that we don't feel very good about ourselves. Some form of blackness has gotten a foothold some- where, and we need to focus our attention on it.

Rachel, the mother of three grown children, realized that most of her time was spent either feeling guilty about the way she had raised them, or trying to make them feel guilty that they hadn't fulfilled all her expectations.

She explained, "I realized that the only way for me not to feel guilty was to make *them* feel guilty. *Somebody* had to feel guilty; that's the way I was raised. Better them than me— except then I didn't want to see them hurt, so I'd take back the guilt myself. It was crazy.

"Finally I took the big step and decided to see what would happen if we just took the whole guilt thing out of the equa- tion, so *nobody* had to feel guilty. I have to tell you it was very strange at first for all of us and it didn't happen over- night. We all felt uneasy because it was so different. But now we're getting used to it and we like it better."

As Rachel suggests, it takes an act of will to get rid of guilt . . . supported by a steady practice of personal awareness.

### THE SMART DIS-EASE

It often seems that people who are particularly "smart," who have had the most success in their intellectually oriented educational system, are the most prone to negativity. Often there is a sniper effect; they subtly put down others— "put them in their place"—as if pushing others down will make them more successful. As I described in "The Tough One," they can't resist taking potshots disguised as humor when in fact they are demeaning others' abilities or skills. When this is pointed out, they often reply "I was only joking!" These are learned behaviors, and "smart" people are good at learning, but I think it goes deeper than that.

Our schools and society promote analytical left-brain thinking, and some intellectually astute people get so in the habit of thinking only with the scientific, rational part of their minds that they develop an extremely critical, analytical approach to everything. They have a mind-set that challenges any new person or idea: "Prove to me that you're worthwhile." They immediately examine any new idea for all the reasons that it won't work, and bombard the person who suggested it with all the rational reasons why it will fail. They toss a wet blanket over the idea before anyone has a chance to consider that it might work or be valuable. With its possibilities cut down by cynicism, the idea never has a chance to germinate.

We all know people who operate like this. Nothing is ever good enough. Nothing ever meets with their wholehearted approval. They can always see something that will go wrong, and that is where they focus. At best, such people acknowledge that something just might be acceptable, but they make sure we know that there is also much to criticize.

The emphasis on rational, scientific inquiry fosters this attitude of negation. If you ask these people to a movie, they either don't want to see it because it hasn't gotten good reviews, or they go with you and rip it to shreds. The dinner was good, but too bad the vegetables weren't hot. They want to lose weight, but they "can't" because people are always forcing them to go out and eat fattening things. They make a full-time occupation out of poking holes in things and cutting people down to size. "Yes, that woman is nice, but too bad she never accomplished much in her life." "Yes, that man has a good business but he's really not very nice."

It's as if they're afraid that if they ever let anything get by without pointing out its faults they wouldn't appear smart enough, or discriminating enough, or astute enough. This habit often gets started because people don't really feel very good about themselves, and school is an area in which they've achieved success and won approval. They feel most comfortable in this intellectual, highly critical arena. It's their turf. It's where they win, where they look good, and where they feel worthwhile and valuable.

Often, when these people start practicing a form of inner focusing, they discover creative parts of themselves that are worthwhile, valuable, and lovable. They find they can afford to relax a bit, and accept things and people who are less than perfect. No longer must they push others down to feel up. They begin using and appreciating life with their right brains as well as with their left brains, and find out that adding the right brain makes them not only smarter and more creative, but more accepting. They are not so afraid of saying "I don't know; let's find out." For the first time, they begin to develop an internal unity and balance. They discover that they don't have to give up the intellectual life at all; they can *enhance* it with a more intuitive, imaginative, and creative side of themselves that also lets them enjoy life more and be more expressive.

*ETHEL'S STORY*

Ethel had worked in public relations in New York for twenty years, moving to San Diego when her husband was transferred. For the first year, being in California made her crazy. She thought everyone she met was a "fuzz-brain." No one read the papers, no one read books, they didn't know what was going on in the world—and what was worse, they didn't seem to care. They talked about their feelings, watched sunsets, and ate kiwi fruit. They seemed to have no logical functioning and were completely undiscriminating in their artistic tastes. Ethel was sure no one in the state had an IQ of more than 80. It's not too hard to see her negative taproot.

But what really made Ethel nuts was the way people talked about their "processes." They loved to remember things that happened when they were children and go over all the feelings they had, all the anger and hurt, and talk about how that might have affected they way they were today. They just couldn't seem to get enough of it. Every time Ethel heard one of these conversations, she blew her stack. It seemed so juvenile, so stupid, so weak and wishy-washy.

In fact, Ethel herself had had a very painful childhood. Her parents had been involved in a very unpleasant divorce and she had felt torn between them, never feeling as if she had a home with either of them. The thought of going back and allowing herself to experience those feelings was terrifying. The thought that they might have something to do with the rather harsh person she had become made her question her identity and feel out of control.

No wonder it made her so uncomfortable when people talked about these feeling-oriented, "airy-fairy" things. Ethel liked objective things that could be measured, understood, and eliminated if they didn't measure up or make sense. The things these people were talking about were subjective and didn't really make sense. They seemed to turn her world upside down.

Nevertheless, Ethel's education and intelligence worked in her favor. She began to realize that, if she had such a strong and actually irrational response to something, she should probably examine it. She took the time to look at why these types of conversations upset her so, realized that they were triggering some of her old emotions, and began taking steps to deal with her issues of abandonment and anger. She began to find words for her feelings.

As she continued to include a daily time of Mind Fitness, Ethel began to see other ways of viewing herself. She realized that she didn't need to rely entirely on her left brain; she could allow some of the softer, more intuitive, emotional parts of herself to surface. She began to feel less threatened, and therefore to be less critical. She began to understand that past events didn't have to dictate who she was; that she was now an adult and could choose her own set of attitudes and responses to life.

People who fall prey to negativity because they are so smart and well educated in analytical skills are usually also smart enough to eventually see what it is doing to them, and to understand that they don't have to be negative and unhappy just because they have been blessed with high intelligence.

## THE PAYOFFS

Why do we behave in ways that actually help to sabotage us? What could we possibly get out of letting ourselves drift into these negative states? Could there actually be payoffs for being so out of balance and miserable?

It's not easy to look at what these payoffs might be; in fact, it can be downright embarrassing, even to ourselves. But the advantage to discovering the payoffs is that we can make choices. We can see if the payoffs are really worth it, or if we're just operating on automatic, based on past needs that aren't relevant now. We can examine whether we get as much from the payoffs as we might if we gave up the particular symptoms that we manifest and lived more fully and joyfully.

Each one of us has different payoffs for different symptoms. We have all adapted our own forms of personal negativity to fit our own perceived "needs" and to ensure our own emotional survival. It may look different in each of us, but there are three common threads that run through most people's negativity payoffs:

1. **Avoiding responsibility.** There is no need to do anything or risk anything if someone or something else is always to blame. By blaming everything outside of ourselves, in a constant stream of whines, complaints, and angry jabs, we put off from ourselves any responsibility for change or positive actions and place it firmly on the shoulders of the outside world. Who are we? Just poor little us. We have no control. With this thinking, we can justify lazy inertia rather than risk taking actions; we can justify complaining rather than creating, anger rather than peace.

2. **Avoiding commitment.** As long as we see the world filled with impossibilities, we don't have to work very hard, to commit to anything, or to demonstrate our abilities. Our attitude is "why run the race if you aren't going to win it?" We never have to fail if we avoid committing to challenges. It's not going to work anyway, so why try? To commit ourselves to a goal means taking a position that requires sustained energy and proactive strategies for success. Saying "why bother?" gets us out of a lot of work, keeps us from stretching our limits, and feeds into a lazy and self-centered mind-set.

3. **Avoiding intimacy.** Staying prickly, irritated, and sullen allows us to hide from others and stay sealed off in our own little world. We don't have to face the challenges of sharing ourselves and being vulnerable if we are always "looking down our noses on others," finding no one else worthy of our respect. Being superior is a sure way of remaining separate. Being intimate with someone would mean we are willing to be equal with others in a respectful and exchanging manner. If we push others away, we can stay noninvolved; we don't have to act on behalf of anyone but our own self-centered selves. Negativity allows us to avoid connecting with others and to stay locked in our own self-justifying and blaming mind-set.

We all have our own personal ways of expressing negativity and our own combination of payoffs, but it's a good bet that most of the symptoms stem from one or more variations of these three. Recognizing this is critical to growth and healing, but we must not make this recognition one more cause for self-recrimination—we must keep in mind that these developed patterns of personal negativity are ways of protecting ourselves, of coping with emotional pain or stress.

### CHOOSING YOUR OWN FOCUS

In this chapter, we've discussed how these habit patterns may have gotten started, and some of the specific symptoms. It's unlikely that anyone manifests *all* these symptoms; some may have symptoms that are not mentioned here. This list is only a guideline to help identify the specific areas on which to focus as we get ready to heal our patterns of defeated thinking. The important thing is for each of us to identify the aspects of our lives that we want to start healing, and to keep those areas in mind as we learn more about this condition and how to reverse it.

# Chapter 6

## *GETTING READY*

Healing, and learning to see with the power of optimism, begin the moment we recognize our negative patterns and make a choice to break that cycle. This is the hardest part—looking directly at our own attitude and realizing that we have played a part in it. We are not out of control after all. The Up Side is that once we know what we are doing, we can opt to learn new ways of behaving . . . at least most of the time.

### *THREE STAGES OF CHANGE*

We can heal personal negativity by taking three steps:
1. *Identify* what is wrong.
2. *Accept and forgive* ourselves for not being perfect.
3. *Heal* the condition.

Let's look at each of these steps.

**1. Identify.** To some people, this seems like an unnecessary step. We already know what's wrong: *we feel awful.* Our lives are not working

However, negativity shows up differently in each of us. We need to do our own soul-searching to pinpoint exactly how it manifests in each of our lives. The clearer we get, the easier it will be to heal the condition. What *exactly* is wrong? Make it clear to yourself exactly what you wish to heal.

Another reason it's important to be specific about what feels out of balance is that many of the forms of limited and fearful thinking tend to be "hidden." They are subtle and insidious, and usually exist for years before we recognize them. And because there has been no name until now, it has been difficult to get a handle on anything meaningful. Acknowledging negatives has not been a part of our culture—something that people share with one another—and so most of us have hidden a lot of these subtle, and not-so-subtle, negative feelings for fear of being criticized or all alone. Now we are discovering that this affects people in all walks of life and at every level of success.

People have found the following questions helpful in identifying just how the taproot of this condition shows up in their lives:

- Am I more unhappy than happy?
- Do I feel angry or upset even when, in reality, my physical environment is acceptable?
- Do I overreact to people who do not agree with me?
- Do I snap at people unnecessarily on some days, and seem much more patient on others?
- Do I wake up in the morning feeling stressed out before I even open my eyes, without even pausing to ask myself how I really feel?
- Do I wonder if I will be able to get through each day?
- Do I feel rushed most of the time?
- Am I more able to keep myself together with strangers than I am with my family? Am I generally inconsistent in my moods and interactions with people?
- Do I sleep more than I really need to, just sit staring into space feeling down and sluggish, or work more than I need to, and in a pressured way?
- Do I feel picked on, abused by life?
- Do I feel sad, complaining, or judgmental more often than the conditions in my life warrant?

- Do I find it difficult to focus my attention and activities, and often feel scattered and incomplete?
- Do I feel tense, anxiously "fighting the clock" most of the time?
- Are most of my first impressions and reactions to people, situations, or new ideas negative?
- Do I feel nothing is ever good enough?
- Is my vocabulary more hostile than gentle? What kinds of words do I use most frequently? Are they supportive, expansive words, or are they more shut down, pessimistic, angry, or defeatist?
- Do I replay negative, upsetting scenes in my mind, feeling more and more angry or powerless but not actually doing anything?

You may answer "No" to all of these questions, and still feel that you suffer from a part of destructive negativity moods and attitudes. If you don't feel these questions have identified exactly how it manifests in your life, take a few minutes now to jot down some of your own ideas.

**2. Accept and Forgive.** The second step is to stop self-justification, to admit we're not perfect, and to forgive ourselves for this. We *do* have some negative, self-defeating attitudes and behaviors that are causing us to live less fulfilling lives than we otherwise would—and we can change these negative, self-defeating attitudes and behaviors.

It's easy to blame others by saying, "I'm the way I am because of how my parents raised me. If they'd done things differently, I'd have a happier, more productive life" or "If I hadn't been abused, I would be softer and gentler," or "If had hadn't been abandoned I could trust more."

It's easy to say, "I can't help it that I've had a tragic life—those things just happened and I was the victim of Fate."

It's easy to say, "If my neighborhood had been better and my parents had had a good relationship, then I'd be able to have one too," or "If my parents had taught me about money, I wouldn't be having all these problems."

Life might indeed be easier given different "what-ifs," and causes beyond our control may seem to take us off the hook, but denial and excuses only prolong negative thinking, making it more difficult for us to do anything about the situation now. If we keep placing blame outside of ourselves, we know that we are still in denial. We can choose to play an active role in *un*-creating our excuses and replacing them with new, more positive attitudes and behaviors. We do this as we accept that our foundation attitudes are learned and created by us, and therefore we can learn new ones.

We can't always control what happens in our lives, but we do have choices about how we *react* to what happens. Life does throw *some* "wild cards" at us—and we cope as best we can. As we all know from our own experiences with personal loss and tragedy, disagreement, separation, and death are painful parts of life. The challenge is to not let them defeat us, but to draw from them renewed meaning for growth and deeper compassion in our lives.

As we begin taking responsibility for our part in our negativity, it's helpful to ask these questions:

- Am I filling my life with more difficulties or blame than I really need to?
- Might some of my problems be self-inflicted?
- Could I have reacted more positively to some of the major changes that have taken place in my life? Is it possible that I've been harboring resentments for a long time?
- Now that I think about it, did I spend quite a bit of time as a youngster imagining negative scenes in my mind?
- Do I let myself dwell on thoughts and feelings that aren't conducive to happiness or growth?
- Do I find it hard to feel happy?

Once we have identified the problem and accepted that we have a part in it, we can begin the process of healing.

**3. Heal.** We make a choice to heal; that is, we set our mind to learning new, more positive attitudes and behaviors. We do this by first taking responsibility for our own moods and attitudes, and then *consciously and actively* employing the same techniques that we have used unconsciously to set these patterns in motion. We put our mind into training. This is a philosophy and way of living based on self-esteem and belief in ourselves and our experiences. It is a new way of thinking about ourselves and what is possible for us based on optimism and self-determination.

"It means:

- Actively listening to our intuition—the quiet inner self that is wiser than the outer, surface self could ever be
- Shifting our thinking from snap judgments and automatic reactions to fuller, richer ways of looking at and reacting to things
- Consciously clarifying and focusing on who we want to be and how we want to live our lives
- Seeing life from a new perspective, based on love and growing, rather than on helplessness, anger, and fear"

Healing, in this book, means removing the fear-based, negative "That won't work . . . they are to blame . . . I can do it better" filter that has colored our perceptions of everything in life, and seeing with optimism, expansion and possibility. It means focusing on the up side by seeing the very best potential in ourselves and others. This is not an overnight process, but we can do it when we chose to begin.

*THE MOMENT OF DECISION*

There comes a moment when we recognize the stranglehold that negative attitudes and thinking have on our lives.

At that point, we have to decide what, if anything, we are going to do about it.

The various forms of personal negativity are habits of fear-based thought. The adrenaline rush we may get from them can make them as addictive as cigarettes, alcohol, drugs, or food. We need just as much courage to overcome habits of negative perception as we do to take on better-known physical addictions.

Most people need time to build up to this moment of decision—the turning point at which we make the commitment to begin to heal ourselves of some of our forms of negativity. But at some point, everything mysteriously comes together and we are ready. It's as if, after being heated for some time, the water finally starts to boil. All our energies seem to come together. We are very clear on what we want, and we muster the courage, the commitment, the will, and the strength to make that decision last through all the temptations that come up.

Our habits of negative thinking have been built up over many years, and they aren't going to disappear overnight. What we are talking about here is not a promise that self-defeating thoughts will never surface again, but a commitment to ourselves to work with them when they do—a commitment to make the effort to learn something from each experience, while focusing on teaching ourselves more empowered thinking. It's an attitude-to-action approach.

Most of us have made some sort of commitment similar to this. It may have concerned an addiction or a relationship or a behavior pattern. When it is time to move on something, there is a moment of drawing in the breath, straightening the spine, and letting a strong determination rise to the surface: a determination to give up some form of self-sabotage, no matter how uncomfortable that may make us in the short term; a determination to relinquish parts of our less-evolved natures for a fuller knowledge and appreciation of our higher possibilities. It is a moment of deep faith in ourselves, a moment of radical trust, a moment of surrender and acceptance that sometimes gives us the feeling of being out of control. The irony, of course, is that in making this commitment to ourselves we gain more control over our lives than we have ever had.

One thing that makes us resist the commitment is that human beings don't like change—even good change. It's uncomfortable not to be who we always were, even if our expansion lets us experience and enjoy life more fully. To break out of one way of doing things and cross over into another is a risky, scary thing to do. It takes great personal courage.

When the change has to do with growth, it's even scarier. When we admit that we want to get better, there's an implication that things aren't so good now. If friends start to say, "You look more relaxed than I've ever seen you before," we have to admit that we looked tense and uptight in the past. If they say, "Hey, you look wonderful!" we suspect that maybe we didn't look so good before.

We can also get caught up in the syndrome of "As long as I stay just mediocre, I won't be noticed." A woman from Ohio once told me she was afraid to dress really nicely because she would look "too sexy and good and then people would notice me. I never know what to say when people make a fuss over me." She was embarrassed by the attention she'd gotten when she dressed well, and felt she didn't know how to handle public admiration, so she hid behind dowdy, nondescript clothes.

There are ways to hide that don't involve clothing. We hide from things we fear. We may hide from commitment, from standing out, from intimacy, from having to admit that we weren't perfect before. That's why it takes such great courage to make a commitment to ourselves—to risk breaking out of the habit of defeat, blame, and anger to create a fuller way of living for ourselves. There are parts of ourselves that would rather be comfortable with what we know, and that don't want us to make the leap to being a self-actualized person who feels fulfilled and successful in life. It takes breaking out of our laziness and sustaining a committed energy for our own well-being and health.

The author and lecturer Hugh Prather reminded us how strong that pull to the negative is, when he said in one of his talks "The ego loves to be a martyr." We need to acknowledge and be gentle with those parts of ourselves, but also to know that we've decided not to let them hold us back.

# PART TWO

## MIND FITNESS FOR HEALING

We are now expanding our thinking as individuals and as a society to recognize that care and "exercise" for the mind is as essential for human health and well-being, as is care and exercise for the body.

# Chapter 7

# *MAGIC WORD #1: RELAXATION*

We can't get far if our mind and body are going in different directions. The best way to bring them together is to breathe deeply and relax.

Our realization of the importance of relaxation is evidenced by an entire new branch of medicine that deals with this mind and body state. Being relaxed doesn't mean being sleepy; it just means freeing the body and mind from unnecessary tensions and distractions, allowing them to quiet down and enter a state of balance, creating a positive effect.

In the classic book *The Relaxation Response*, Dr. Herbert Benson of Harvard Medical School points out that relaxation benefits both the mind and the body, and that relaxing one tends to relax the other. As our minds quiet down, our bodies relax more. As our bodies relax more, our minds become more calm. The point of relaxation is to ease tension and quiet the action in both our bodies and minds so that the more subtle forms of thinking can take place. There are many ways this can be done.

*Breathing is the physical technique used most often to help us relax.* Relaxation takes place naturally as we simply pay attention to our breath flowing in and out, in and out. Try it now. As you breathe in, let the breath travel down into your abdomen rather than staying in the chest area as it usually does. Hold it for a few seconds, and slowly release the air in a long steady stream. Repeat this slow abdominal breathing three to five times, and feel how your body naturally begins to release tension that has been stored in the muscles. Feel the tension flowing out of your body on the exhalation.

This technique can be practiced anywhere, at any time, to release stored-up tension. By now it is no secret that medical science believes that much of our illness and disease is caused by the constant tension that we store in our bodies. We still react to stressful situations with the adrenaline-pumping "flight or fight" response of our early ancestors. They could use all that adrenaline to either kill or run away from a mastodon, but we can't do either if we're sitting in gridlocked traffic. Each time we consciously relax with this simple breathing exercise, we de-tense our bodies and minds, lessen toxins, and actively do something to become more relaxed, calmer, and healthier.

This relaxed state shifts our attention from the outer world to our inner world. It restores our balance both physiologically and psychologically, and gives us a chance to rest.

## PEACE AND QUIET

We might say to a child who wants to tell us a story, "Wait until I can sit down and really listen to you." In much the same way, we need to take time out and consciously relax in order to hear our own inner intuitive voice.

Relaxation prepares our bodies and minds for learning, creating, and performing. As we quiet the chatter of thoughts, deepen and slow down our breathing, and release tension in all parts of our body, we begin to feel calm, quiet, and serene, at peace with ourselves and the world.

In this alert, wakeful but restful state of relaxation, we are most open to receiving new thoughts and developing images in a way that we are not when we are more active and responding to outside pressures. All our attention is focused inward. Our eyes are usually closed, we aren't moving around doing things, and we are centered in the imaginative and feeling parts of ourselves. This is the place of power in which our images have the greatest power to actually affect what happens in our lives.

### THE INNER VOICE

An inner voice symbolically represents the whisperings that we can hear when we sit quietly and focus on our own thoughts and feelings. These thoughts and feelings spring from deep within ourselves rather than in reaction to outside events in our lives. They come from our center. A quiet voice is just that . . . it is quiet. We rarely hear it when we are in a hurry or getting dinner ready or doing homework with our children.

The intuitive voice takes many forms, from a flash of insight or a gut-level hunch to a full-blown confidence that *this* is what we should be doing. It is that part of us that sees and feels the whole of a situation and responds from that higher level of awareness.

The intuitive sense signals our deepest inclinations from within, with a feeling of "That's the right thing for me do to" or "Yes, this is what I want to do." Unlike your rational, left-brain consciousness—which responds to all the outside 'shoulds'—your intuitive sense is in touch with what is called "emotional literacy": the awareness of your own deepest feelings and desires about how you can uniquely live your own life. Your intuitive sense is your own individual sense of direction—a tool of the soul. When you use your quiet time to connect with this inner sense, you can begin to recognize your true desires, and to make them a reality.

When you follow your intuition, you become a pioneer: venturing out into the unknown, the uncharted waters of your own psyche; endeavoring to follow your own inner guidance rather than relying on what others may be telling you about what you should be doing.

It is transforming to relate to the intuition when you express yourself in an artistic work. For years I took classes in my art field, and did some fine work, yet only when I listened to my own intuitive voice—which encouraged me to work on my own for a year or so without taking classes or instruction—was I able to shed outside influence and develop my own unique style of work. It takes courage to "go off by yourself and listen within," but it is well worth the journey.

When we heed that inner sense, we may discover that long-sought-after solutions suddenly and spontaneously spring to mind. We have moved from one mode of thinking to another—a deeper, almost mysterious sense of thinking. These answers may come right after we have been focusing intensely on them in our conscious, thinking mind, and have then simply let go and entered a state of relaxation and meditation.

You will know when it's your intuitive voice speaking to you: It is quiet and gentle, rather than loud and pushy, and it contains a gem of wisdom that you may have missed before.

**A major theme of the Mind Fitness philosophy is that it's very important to honor the process of inner being by setting up specific times when we stop all our other activities and change our focus to internal quiet through relaxation.**

### A QUIET PLACE

The practice of relaxation and inner listening is easier if we have an imaginary special place within us to which we go. I call this the "personal template of relaxation." It is really just a place that we imagine within ourselves, with all the sensations we feel when we are in that place. It might be a beach, the top of a mountain, a sunlit meadow, a comfortable living room, a forest, lake, or river, or just a hammock in the garden.

Take a few minutes to imagine a place that you know and love. Imagine an environment where you feel at peace, comfortable, and serene. Feel the calmness of relaxation wash over you. This is the place where you will mentally begin your time-out session each day—your inner retreat ritual. It may take a few days to get used to this being your quiet mental place. (You are free to choose a new relaxation place at any time.) Each time you revisit a mental image of your special place, you will relax more quickly and easily.

It's also helpful to set up a special physical place in your home for your mental reflection exercises. Just taking the time to establish this as your place is meaningful. You are telling yourself that you have made a decision to heal and grow by spending some time in proactive reflection and quiet.

Some people are able to set aside an entire room as their place for inner mind work. When we lived in Hawaii, we had a small room that we used for this purpose. It was the "quiet room." We went there to do our inner work and whenever we felt the need to be calm and at peace spiritually. In that room, we felt protected until we could find a fuller light within ourselves. (Sometimes when we were hosting a party, I would discover a guest hidden away in the quiet room.) It was a place to reach decisions simply by relaxing and reflecting. The little room reminded us, by its very presence, to take time for inner work, and it gave us a safe haven during the process.

Most people use part of a room, perhaps a corner or shelf, for their special place. Now that we live in a smaller house, I use a small chest on which I place things that are meaningful to me. Each of us can create a special place that is our personal temple. In our special place we each can have symbols that inspire us: pictures, statues, flowers, shells, prayers, written affirmations, crystals, and personally meaningful tokens.

Each time we walk by our quiet place, we are reminded of our dedication to expanding our lives and fulfilling our highest potential. We're also reminded of the larger universe and our relation to the whole.

When I travel, I take a special place with me. I carry a small scarf to act as a table covering, a few pictures of my family, and some of the items from my special place at home. I find that no matter where I am, as soon as I set up my special place, I have a wonderful sense of being grounded and at home.

My husband took a few special objects and pictures to Moscow with him and set them up on the night stand in his hotel room. The next day, he came back in the middle of the afternoon to find three of the floor women gathered in his room looking at his special place and admiring the objects he had there. They were very embarrassed and scurried out quickly, but later one of them came back and apologized. She spoke a bit of English and said, "This is very special to you, no?" He replied with a simple "Yes." From that day on, despite the fact that it was the middle of February and flowers were expensive and hard to find in Moscow, a fresh flower was always placed on his table.

There is a certain power in ritual. At night, before going to sleep, I often light a candle briefly. It's a personally meaningful time for me to remember why I'm here, a time to join myself with the Divine by whatever name, to step back from the day and take a breath that allows images of quiet into my mind and heart. I am reminded that fire is something that human beings have shared for millennia. For thousands and thousands of years, people of our planet have looked into the center of this life-giving element and experienced a sense of wonder at its warmth and light. This simple practice invites me to feel united with a greater whole and a consciousness that is growing and expanding.

## A RELAXATION MEDITATION

This is a meditation that people have found useful for relaxation. It is a good tool, especially if you record it slowly on a tape recorder and play it back to yourself. We all have our own ways of finding that relaxed state, and this may serve as a guide:

*I am taking the time to sit down and relax now because I know that it is good for me. It's something that not only brings me pleasure and peace of mind, but is also very good for my body. I quiet my mind, my breathing becomes deeper and fuller, my heart beats at a slower pace, and I can feel my muscles loosening, reaching a place of quiet and ease.*

*I am taking this quiet time each day to improve my health and well-being, and to welcome new thoughts and feelings that are beneficial to me. This is the time that I can fill my mind with thoughts of fullness, of my dreams for myself. It is also the time when my mind can just rest in the quietness that brings insight and creative thoughts—as pictures, as sensations, or as words.*

*As I take a deep breath, I feel the flood of quietness reach every part of my body. I imagine a golden, honey-colored light pouring down through the top of my head and I feel release as the light touches my eyes, melting all the tension, and down my cheeks and through my mouth, throat, and neck, inviting me to give in to its warmth and release the tightness in my shoulders, down my arms, wrists, and fingertips.*

*I draw in another deep and full breath, shifting the breathing from my chest to my lower abdomen. I breath in again deeply, hold the air in my abdomen for a few moments, and then slowly let it out. I feel the richness of the quiet moment alive within me. I allow the quieting to move through my chest, back, stomach, and lower intestines, down through my groin, legs, and feet—relaxing, letting go of all tensions.*

*As I take in another deep breath, I can feel the increased oxygen circulating through my brain. I call on the power of my concentrated mind to focus in on one thing and to hold that point for as long as I can. I am going to focus in on an image of a quiet pond, a pond that has a large full tree standing on its shore, with cattails and other reeds growing around it. The pond is totally serene and quiet. There are no ripples on its surface. It is completely quiet and tranquil. I soften the light and inhale a sweet scent as I fill my mind with images of this pond. I let go of any other thoughts I may have, focusing on tranquility of mind and relaxation of body.*

*I know that as I focus on the pond and its stillness, my mind will stop whirling around and will come to rest in the center of me, providing me with a rest so that I can accomplish all my needs better and faster after my relaxation and peace.*

*I take in another deep breath and let go of any tensions my body may still be holding as I reflect once again on the pond and its quietness—the beauty of the water's reflection, the fullness of the green tree, and the gentleness of the reeds as they grow near the water's edge.*

*My image for my relaxed body is that of a sleeping cat, totally at peace with the world, purring in its most contented way, not a tight muscle anywhere. My body becomes like a cat's—loose, limp, totally at one with the world around me. Every part of my body feels heavy as I release any desire to move.*

*It is from this quiet place within my mind and body that I can feel the inner voice beginning to rise up into my awareness. I feel that presence of wholeness, of beauty, of total tranquility. I feel that bubble of spirit rise up, giving new meaning to everything I had been worried about during the day. This clear bubble that I imagine is a spiritual essence within me that seems to unite my body, mind, and heart.*

*I ask in this place of quietness for guidance about how to live my life, how to solve my problems, and how to best be of service. I take in another deep breath, knowing that I have taken quiet time to nourish myself, to connect my body and spirit. I know that my body heals itself, that my mind reaches a point of clarity, and that my spirit touches the source of life.*

*I feel myself awakening to the reality around me. I begin to wiggle my fingers and toes, take in a deep breath, slowly open my eyes, and feel refreshed and unified in body, mind, and heart, knowing that I did something good for myself today.*

# Chapter 8

# *MAGIC WORD #2: VISUALIZATION*

Visualization means using the mind's eye to paint a picture of a desired result. When we visualize, we actually create an experience in our imaginations, using as many senses as possible: sight, hearing, touch, smell, and taste. The result can be more positive attitudes and states of mind, a good grade on a test, an athletic performance, healing from an illness—quite literally, anything we can imagine.

Imaging is the very core of the active part of Mind Fitness training. It is basic to changing any habit or learning any new skill. We must be able to imagine the change in order to create it. Carl Jung wrote, "But what great thing came into existence that was not first fantasy? All the works of humanity have their origin in creative imagination. . . . Fantasy is a natural and vital activity which helps the seeds of development to grow."

Anything we create has to exist first in our mind's eye. We can't create or change anything unless we can imagine it first. Imagining ourselves functioning optimally helps us to be that way. The activity comes to life first in the mind.

By creating pictures and feelings of our goals in our minds, we move from vague, abstract desires to more concrete planning. This translation from abstract to concrete gives the Mind Fitness process its power.

One thing that makes visualization so effective is that it

uses part of the mind-brain system in which mental images are born. In Western society we are trained to use our analytical, logical, language-oriented mind-brain systems, so this focus on the imaginative function represents a shift.

We need to urge ourselves gently away from the predominantly rational, spoken-word world in which we live every day, and refocus our attention on the more diffuse and subtle energies that make up our imagination.

We may feel silly at first, sitting with our eyes closed and calling up images of how we would like our lives to be, how we would like to feel. We've been cautioned about "daydreaming" and never taught that it's all right—much less desirable—to spend time each day "doing nothing" (doing nothing but taking an active role in creating our futures!) However, times are changing and our new research indicates that biopsychology—the interplay between the mind and body—is a growing field. Rollo May emphasizes this changing perception when he asks, "What if imagination and art were not the frosting at all, but the fountainhead of human experience?"

As we give ourselves permission to drift in that intuitive, creative, nonlinear, right-brain part of ourselves, we begin to feel more comfortable and receptive there. We begin to touch a new spiritual part of our human experience. Now we can start to draw from that right brain the mental pictures and feelings that will focus us on how we want to be.

*MIND AND BODY*

Visualization not only enhances memory and creativity, it also improves physical performance. When we imagine ourselves performing an action such as playing tennis, the picture in our mind actually fires the brain's neurons to activate the muscles we would use in that activity. As we imagine the perfect tennis stroke, tiny impulses are sent to the exact muscles we would use to make that motion. It's as if we actually took the swing in miniature. We may actually feel the muscle twitch, or feel nothing, but a pattern has been established in our body duplicating that perfect tennis stroke.

When we repeat the images, the pattern continues to build between the mind and body. When we actually get out on the tennis court, we find that our stroke has improved. We have been practicing it with our minds, and also with our bodies, without ever leaving the house.

The same principle holds true for all physical activities. That is why simply watching a video of a perfect golf swing with active attention will actually improve one's golf game.

### USING ALL THE SENSES

The word visualization is partially a misnomer, because we don't just use our visual sense. The more senses we can involve in our imaging, the better—hearing, seeing, feeling, smelling, tasting, or a combination. The goal is to create the illusion of actually being there, doing the activity or existing in the state of mind that we imagine.

Visualization isn't just thinking about something. There is a difference between thinking and imaging. Imaging means *involvement* in the activity—allowing ourselves to feel the emotions, heightening the physical sensations and making them as real as possible—being mentally proactive. The most powerful images are vivid ones that involve all the senses and bring the emotions into play. In visualization, the mind becomes a canvas on which we experiment with painting and sensing various forms and colors. The wider our range of colors and senses, the greater the range of possibilities open to us.

### PASSIONATE ENERGY

Visualization is an *active* process. Imaging doesn't just happen to us; it takes personal motivation and a high level of commitment to ourselves. We must *do something*. Whether we want to heal our unloving thinking patterns, lose five pounds, hit a baseball better, close a business deal, or pass a test, we must commit clear, strong energy to our goal.

Winners in all fields share one characteristic: They have a passion for their goals. They are so involved with what they are doing that they visualize their goals all the time, without even having to think about them. That's just where their minds naturally gravitate. The successful lawyer can't stop thinking about his cases; the golfer's happiest moments off the course are spent fantasizing the perfect swing; the artist wakes up visualizing her next creation; the pregnant woman daydreams constantly about loving a healthy, happy baby.

These people visualize and experience the results they want on deep mental and emotional levels. They *live* their visualizations, even if they are driving along the freeway or sitting in a movie theater when the images occur. They are obsessed with their visions in a positive way, so they spend a lot of time living in their minds' eyes the experiences of success.

We can do the same thing with personal negative thinking patterns. **The key here is to focus not on the negativity itself, but on the constructive feelings and behaviors we want to create in our moment-to-moment lives.** It's hard to get positively excited about obsessive hostile thoughts. Until now, we may have been in the habit of obsessing about negative things, of concentrating all our energy, our dreams, and our images on what was *wrong*. A friend was telling me how her mind seemed to be powerfully pulled like "a leaf in a current towards thinking the worst thoughts possible. When I was told about a lump in my breast I had to pull my thoughts with real determination away from drifting back to the worst possibilities."

Until now, you may have been pulled unknowingly into a

habit of obsessing about the worst possibilities, concentrating your energy, your dreams and your images on what was wrong. Your mind may just seem to gravitate toward the negative. Now, let's at least give those automatic thoughts some competition! To do that, we want to actively visualize something we *can* get excited about—a more loving and nurturing way of relating to ourselves; a stronger self-image of the things we want to do with our lives; deeper, more intimate relationships. Let's take the focus off of the external, and what is not right.

We want to become proactive and directive in turning a recognized negative attitude into something more empowering. Each time we catch ourselves getting lost in negative ideas, daydreaming about our unworthiness or being a victim, we need to say "*Stop!*" After we stop, we need to find another, more positive image with which to replace the old one. We need to *step in actively*, stop the automatic thinking pattern, and then take definite, concrete steps to replace it with positive images. It's a self-directed "stop and about-face" when we find the mind obsessing—replacing that kind of old worn-out thinking with a kind that we consciously choose. Sometimes it works, sometimes it doesn't—but at least we are no longer just running on automatic reactions with their endlessly repeated mental cycles. We have a tool to help us move into a thinking pattern that is more empowering and healthful in the long run.

Learning a new habit starts with creating the new situation in our own mind and heart. We have to see the new behavior in our mind before we can actually demonstrate and live it.

Several months after Jim began his proactive reflections, he still found himself worrying compulsively about his freelance photography business. He had several regular clients and had been successful on his own for two years, but Jim harbored fears of all his business drying up overnight. He even extended this fantasy to an image of himself as a "bag man" with no money and no place to stay, sleeping in the park.

Jim's friends laughed, because he looked so successful to them and they couldn't imagine him on the streets, but the fantasy was very real to him. Although phobic fears are rarely based on reality, that does not diminish their power over the individual. This vision of poverty was so strong, in fact, that Jim often felt overwhelmed by it, powerless to stop it from running over and over in his head.

What finally enabled Jim to conquer his automatic negative imaging was his perseverance and his absolute unwillingness to be defeated by a thinking habit. He made a decision. Each time a fearful fantasy rose in his mind, he stopped whatever he was doing and devoted all of his energy to handling that negative image. He sat down, closed his eyes, and told it to STOP. Sometimes it did right away; sometimes it took a little longer. But Jim never gave up. He kept at it, and gradually he had more and more success making the old habitual fantasy shut down. Eventually, he consciously replaced his negative thoughts with his own vision of what he called "The Other Side."

In this image, all the fear of failure was gone. Jim had gotten to The Other Side of his negative mental habits and was living a life free from worry about business and money. In his imagination, he saw himself shooting pictures in the Himalayas, in Africa, in Japan—all the places he most wanted to visit—and being paid more money than he knew what to do with. He used the same images each time so that they could grow stronger and stronger within him. He let himself *feel* the success, and absorbed those emotions deep within himself. He tasted the exotic foods, smelled the strange, pungent odors of those exciting places, felt the ground under his feet, saw the way the sun shone differently in various places around the world.

The stronger his images of The Other Side became, the

more they eclipsed his old, negative fantasies, which were actually pretty shopworn and not nearly as exciting.

No one else can heal the automatic fear-ridden thoughts that make up the various forms of the disease of negativity for each of us. It's entirely in our hands. As we develop a passionate commitment and desire to kick the habit of automatic fearful thinking, we know that more enlivening thoughts will follow. Remember that for many of us, with our backgrounds of early hurts, loving ourselves is not an automatic response; rather, it is a *learned skill.*

## A PERSONAL PROGRAM

Each of us must take an individualized approach to our Mind Fitness. Only we know what makes us peaceful, relaxed, and fulfilled—and those things are likely to be different for each of us. The images we develop from our creative imaginations will be specifically designed to take each of us where we want to go.

Some of us will start with focusing on a better relationship with our children or our spouse. Others will want a more positive attitude in business. Others will feel the need for a fuller and more rewarding personal life, more friends, perhaps some new creative project. Some of us will just want to stop feeling so tired, grouchy, and pressured all the time. Some will be thinking about dramatic life changes. Others won't want to alter anything, but will want to see and experience everything from a more balanced and optimistic point of view.

Since we are the only ones who know what makes us feel in balance and fulfilled, it's important that we give some attention to what creates that feeling for us. When I pose this question in workshops, a surprising number of people draw a blank. We're not taught to think about what would make us happy, and very few of us actually do. We mull over what makes us *un*happy—and we can often pinpoint what's *wrong* in our lives, making long lists of problems—but very few of us actually sit down and think specifically about the things that would make us feel love and happiness.

Make a list of items that do make your life happy. Close your eyes and get a perfect image of what your life and feelings would be like if you were filled with love and were completely happy. Can you list twenty things?

One woman did this in a workshop and found herself imaging the same attitudes, actions, and behaviors she already had in her life. To her surprise, she was happy exactly as she was! "I discovered that I have been happy and successful all my life," she said, "and I never even knew it!" She changed her self-definition accordingly. Most of us will find that we want to make some changes, but we may also be surprised at how many aspects of our reality resemble our ideal.

## CREATING THE PICTURE

There are two main kinds of imagery: I call them **Memory Images** and **Creative Images**. Memory images are pictures in our minds from the past, such as where and how things are. We use images from our memory every day—to drive to that restaurant where we dined last year, to locate that library book we must return. We recall the pattern of the streets we drove through; we remember where we tend to stash things temporarily in the house. We use memory images when we recall the view from our bedroom window, the sound of someone's voice, or the smell of bread baking in the oven.

The danger inherent in Memory Images is that we can get into the habit of going through day after day using *only* memory, reactivating the same emotions without stopping to consider whether we want them, without remembering that we have it in our power to create new feelings and beliefs. When we fall into the old, self-defeating, pessimistic habits of thought, we're relying only on obsessive memory patterns of thinking. This leaves us playing the same old emotional tapes without creating new ones more fitting, perhaps, for today's reality.

This is not to say that images from the past are not useful: We need them to negotiate in the world, to get from one place to another, to remember how to use the washing machine. They are the guiding thread of our days. However, we don't want to function mostly from memory rather than giving each fresh experience its due. Once we start operating *only* from the past—especially, using memories that promote our version of negativity—we are in trouble.

**Creative Images** are new thoughts—things we've never before thought of in exactly that way; new perceptions and beliefs about ourselves and others. Creative Images come from releasing old memories and images of the past, from forgiving others and ourselves. Creative Images call on the imagination to paint new pictures in our minds. It takes a little more energy to create an image than it does simply to replay the same old pictures, but the rewards are well worth the extra effort. By activating our imaginations and giving them free rein on a regular basis, we can begin to draw ourselves the way we would like to be, imagine the activities that would bring us the most pleasure, and let ourselves feel the emotions that make us feel most alive.

Joseph Campbell, the well-known mythologist, calls this process "Following your bliss." It is the essence of a self-actualized, fully living and loving person.

Now let's look at two kinds of Creative Images: Intuitive Images and Purposeful Images. Purposeful Images are very self-directed, like arrows toward a specific, well-defined goal. I'll talk about these in the next section, and focus first on Intuitive Images.

**Intuitive Images** are not so tightly defined as Purposeful Images; we simply let them bubble up from our intuition. With Intuitive Imaging, we come to our quiet time with no specific goal in mind and simply allow our inner voices to rise to the surface at their own will and speak to us. When we clear the mind and wait quietly for intuitive images or sensations, a special thought, image, or feeling may float to the surface that is more insightful than anything we might have thought with our conscious minds. Sometimes the unconscious has some surprising things to say. More often than not, those things are more important than we might have thought.

Matthew Fox, author and philosopher on the subject of creative spirituality, says that "wisdom requires imagination and nurtures it." He's talking about a coming together of the whole: conscious and unconscious, inner and outer awareness. The quiet part of Mind Fitness encourages such a joining and unity.

At one seminar, Steve described being unhappy for some time about not having a special woman in his life. The rest of his life was going very well: His career as an engineer was taking off, there were no financial worries, he had lots of friends. Yet somehow having a successful relationship had eluded him. This was the area where he concentrated his Mind Fitness program. He had done purposeful imaging on the subject, getting clearer on his values and what he wanted in a relationship. He had asked himself questions. Now he decided to supplement his idealized versions with some Intuitive Images.

But when Steve sat down, cleared his mind, and relaxed his body, and began opening up to whatever Intuitive Images came his way, all he could see was an image of himself playing racquetball. He had played a lot of racquetball several years earlier, when it had been fashionable. But then his career had become more time-consuming and he had gotten involved in bicycling; he hadn't played racquetball since, and had no conscious desire to do so.

Steve let the image go, took another deep breath, and cleared his mind. Again, the image of himself playing racquetball floated to the surface. He gave up on Intuitive Imaging for the afternoon, but later got to thinking that it might be fun to play a few games of racquetball after all. He called his old racquetball partner, Rob, and persuaded him to take a couple of hours off on Saturday afternoon for old time's sake.

They had a good game, and afterward in the juice bar they met a woman named Eileen. Steve has been seeing her ever since.

## IMAGES WITH A PURPOSE

**Purposeful Creative Images** are specifically designed to make something happen. Sometimes people find this a bit intimidating; they fear they "won't be able to come up with any good images" or will "freeze up" when asked to let something entirely new come into their minds. But almost everyone finds the process surprisingly easy with just a little practice. It's as old as "wishing on a star."

First, relax. Take a few deep breaths and let all the tension pour out of your body. Now consciously tell yourself that you are going to visualize yourself doing something you would like to be doing. To get used to doing this, start with something you've done before, rather than with a completely new activity. When you have the picture in your mind, begin filling in more details and making the picture as vivid as possible.

Suppose, for instance, that you create the image of walking on the beach. Imagine your feet on the warm sand as you walk along, enjoying the sound of the waves, the sight of the blue sky, the smell of the seaweed washing up along the shore. Taste the salt in the air as you feel the sea breezes touching your face and arms. Now let these sensations create feelings of joy and pleasure, bubbling up inside as you spread your arms to embrace this moment.

Try this exercise with some other activities you've already experienced, then move on to creating new experiences. Remember, visualization works best when all the senses are brought into play, when you give yourself over emotionally to the experience. The more details you can include, the better. The more fully you can experience the mental and emotional conditions you imagine, the more powerful the imaging will be. It's like "mind drawing," using all of the senses, making your intention very clear to yourself. This helps you recognize it when it comes your way. To define is to create.

One of my first experiences with Purposeful Creative Imagery happened when the house we were renting was sold and we had to move. I decided to imagine in my mind the new home we would find. I took a few relaxing breaths, and started mentally visualizing as if I were drawing.

The kind of house I wanted surfaced immediately in my mind's eye. I saw it bathed in sunshine, not too far from town, on a relatively flat street that allowed for bike riding. I went for the ideal as I mentally drew the living room with a lot of glass and heard the sound of birds singing outside.

Several times a day, I made a point of flashing on that picture in my mind's eye. I approached it each time with total assurance, not allowing any doubts to occupy my mind. I did not permit any negative thoughts that might have made me pessimistic—like the fact that most of the town was extremely hilly and had large redwood trees that shaded most of the homes. I just held steadfastly to the picture I'd created in my mind—as I stepped out of the shower, as I waited at a stop light, as I got in line to buy cat food, as I walked across a room. I flashed on the image as often as I remembered to do so.

Sure enough, within a few months we were living in a home very much like the one I had imagined. It's very simple. When we get defined and clear on what we want, we are more likely to have it come our way. Maybe we just recognize it.

### MIND LIFTS MEANS PUMPING IMAGES

My constant, regular flashing on the image of our ideal new home was one of my most effortless—and effective—experiences of frequent imaging. I kept thinking about it naturally and could easily visualize what we wanted. You can think of these short flashes—brief visions of positive images—like sets of lifting weights or pumping iron, except it's your imagination doing the lifting. I call it Pumping Images, or Mind Lifts.

You can make up your own Mind Lifts and pump whatever images you wish. Here are two, easily adapted, that people find helpful for generally "pumping up" their self-esteem and confidence.

- *Imagine yourself giving a speech, a presentation, or even a dinner. Instead of concentrating on your familiar fears, start to see yourself standing up in front of the group with confidence and enthusiasm. See the size and shape of the room, the kinds of chairs people are sitting in, the kinds of people in the audience. Sense the taste in your mouth, the smells in the room, the sound of applause, and the emotional excitement of making your presentation. Image everything exactly the way you would like it to be, and know that as you do this, you are carrying over the benefits and sense of accomplishment into every area of your life.*

- *Suppose that you would like to have a more interesting job. Imagine exactly what that job would look like. Remember, you are pretending, so make it as ideal as you can. What specific activities are you doing? What are you wearing? How does the work feel? With whom are you working? See the colors of your new surroundings, sense the sounds, the smells, the general atmosphere of the new workplace. See yourself talking with your boss and hearing her praise you for your fine work. Feel your hand in a handshake as you are congratulated for the outstanding contribution you are making. Feel a sense of emotional abundance and wholeness within yourself. Know that anything you can imagine, you can achieve.*

# Chapter 9

## *MAGIC WORD #3: AFFIRMATION*

Affirmations are clear statements that the realities we want are possible, and that we believe we can have them. They are declarations of possibility and trust.

Here are some examples of affirmations that people have created in seminars. These statements help guide their thinking in the direction in which they want it to go. They draw strength and clarity of intention from these personal directives:

- I am learning to say "Yes!"
- I have been successful in my life.
- I believe in and trust myself.
- I am loving myself and others more and more.
- I choose to heal my negative patterns and think supportive, constructive thoughts.
- I accept and forgive myself.
- I am a peaceful, committed person.

Affirmations seem so simple that people sometimes dismiss them as Pollyanna-like, self-deluding chatter that merely works like a placebo—making us feel better, but having no actual effect on reality. People who have fallen prey to the cynical, pessimistic, "guilty until proven innocent" mentality are particularly apt to put down affirmations. Some of this comes from the scientific indoctrination we've all received that tells us that anything so simple, and yet so untouchable and not statistically measurable, has to be stupid.

However, when we understand the power of verbal thinking we begin to understand that the way in which we talk to ourselves, whether in affirming or disrespecting terms, plays a key role in our mental well-being. Our self-definition and the declarations we make to ourselves are very important.

Affirmations have astonishing power, especially when consciously incorporated with images. Linear, left-brain, language-based affirmations are actually a powerful complement to intuitive, right-brain, picture-based images.

## BELIEF IN OURSELVES

A feeling of trust and belief in ourselves is key to good mental health. Affirmations reinforce the belief that we can reach our goals, that we believe in ourselves. They guide our behavior by reminding us of what we value and how we want to be in our lives. By being proactive, we put awareness and thought into our affirmations. We can't just mouth the words and hope for the best; it's essential to put the intentional power of our attention, will, and feelings behind them.

We can all tell the difference between an actor who is simply reading the script and someone who puts feeling and emotional energy into what she is saying. The words delivered with emotion create a spark of feeling within us—sometimes so strong that we have physical reactions, such as tensing our muscles, laughing, or crying. The intention and the active emotional energy behind an affirmation make it powerful.

If for some reason we find it hard really to believe what we're saying in an affirmation, we can stop and examine what specific doubt is undercutting that belief. The important thing is to be aware of our reactions and notice when doubts prevent us from getting behind our beliefs. For instance, if we find ourselves wincing each time we say, "I deserve a job I love," we can stop for a moment and look for the source of that reaction. What is undercutting our belief that we deserve a job we love? We might have bought something that our parents said a long time ago about work being a struggle, not an activity to be enjoyed. Or we might have been told we'd never get a job we liked without certain educational degrees.

Once we know what the barrier is, we can examine it and let it go. It's not true that work has to be drudgery, and once we understand that we've been holding this false belief in our unconscious, we can forgive ourselves and let it go. It's not true that we need certain degrees to enjoy our work, but we might never even have realized that we held that unconscious belief if we hadn't brought it to the surface through examination with affirmations.

Through affirmations, we create the reality in our minds before it actually happens. The more deeply we believe in our ability to reach our goals, the more likely we are to do so. Affirmations guide our perceptions and put us into the "*I can*" mode of thinking.

Willis Harmon wrote in *Higher Creativity*, "Affirmation is a way of reprogramming the unconscious idea and image processor through mental and vocal repetition of the ideas or images which we want our minds to accept as 'input'." We may want to try reprogramming to make these changes:

- Create more positive attitudes.
- Experience more self-confidence and trust.
- Improve our relationships with family and coworkers.
- Develop a new relationship.
- Make more money.
- Experience more passion in life.
- Feel more empowered and personally secure.
- Work up the courage to make a career change.
- Perform a job or sport with more excellence.

In learning to visualize, we've been concentrating on getting in touch with the purposeful and intuitive. Affirmations translate our creative images into meaningful words. We are language-based beings and we need to include language in our learning; affirmations reinforce in words the belief that we can do whatever it is that we are visualizing.

Affirmations also allow us to retrieve images from our unconscious. Language is the set of symbols we use to organize things in our minds. If we want to call up something from our unconscious, we'll have more luck if it has a name. We might say, for instance, "It's time for my relaxation period. I think I'll call up that image I used last time of the pond with the reeds and the glass-like surface." This brings back the meditation we used last time, and gives us access to that part of our unconscious. Words help us proactively guide our thinking patterns. They are the narration of the story and strongly direct our tone and mood. They form an essential part of our attitude, whether positive or negative.

With affirmations, we actually use language to help us move to images—guiding our thinking with the words. To test this, try to image an apple *without* saying the word "apple" in your mind. We use words to label the memory files in our minds for fast, easy retrieval. Affirmations form the bridge between our inner world of visualization and the outer world of physical reality. When we pair word power with emotional feeling and sensory images, we have a tremendously potent force that galvanizes our intentions and ability to create in the world.

### *MAKE THEM YOUR OWN*

It is important to repeat our affirmations regularly, just as it is important to return again and again to the mental images empowering us. We want to *own* these images and words.

Research shows that certain thoughts produce physical changes in our bodies, our brains, our chemistry, and our muscles. Actual physical connections are made among various parts of the brain, and between the brain and the body. The internal structure of our brains is always changing, depending on what we are doing, experiencing, or thinking. Each time we repeat a thought pattern, the brain's physical structure actually changes. Here's how it works:

Our brains are made up of billions of interconnecting neural fibers. The places where these fibers connect are called *synapses*. At each synapse, the electrical impulse generated by the thought has to jump from one piece of neural fiber to the next. Amazingly, each time we think a thought, there is a slight modification in that particular synapse. It's as if a small "groove" is started and the next time we think that same thought, it is easier for the neural impulse to make that same jump again.

Recent research shows that the brain is continually modifying itself. When patterns are repeated, the neural pathways begin to form deeper "grooves" that make the jump easier and easier. That's how we learn to do things automatically. The first time we play a piano piece, our movements may be hesitant and halting, but after repeated practice we can play it "without thinking." In the same way, we hit a tennis ball so often over the years that the motion becomes "automatic."

These grooves may make it difficult to break negative habits, but their presence shows us that we have the power to create new grooves and new habits at any time of life. In *The Brain Book*, Peter Russell says, "Learning almost always results in some of the brain's trillions of synapses changing their ability to transmit impulses." What that means to us is that the more we do or say something, the more our brains changes to accommodate that new pattern of thinking or action. This is the process by which affirmations change not only our thinking, but the actual structure of our brain!

In our eagerness to succeed and move forward, it is sometimes tempting to change directives too quickly. If we don't get results within twenty-four hours, we switch to another set of words. Sometimes the process of making new thoughts our own takes time. If you don't feel good about an affirmation, by all means move on to something else. But it's also important to give a new affirmation some time to settle in and allow the new "grooves" to form. Choose the affirmations that you want, and stick to those same ones for a month or so. Allow each new mind-set to work with your images and pump some feeling into them. Allow them your new reality.

Try turning off the car radio when you drive and using that time to do affirmations. Some people even make tapes of their favorite affirmations to play on the tape deck in the car, leaving about ten seconds between each one so that they can say them aloud as they drive. You can affirm silently in the line at the market, walking down the street, doing the dishes, whenever you have some down mental time that you want to enjoy more and put to good use! This keeps your mind chatter focused in the direction in which you want to go.

### WORDED IN THE POSITIVE

Affirmations are easier for the mind to digest and act on if they are phrased in positive ways. We always get better results when we ask a child (or anyone) to *do* something than when we tell them *not* to do something. Saying "Walk!" is usually more effective than saying, "Don't run!" It's clearer, more positive, and doesn't force him to search through his brain for the opposite of "run." If we create negatively stated affirmations, we force our minds to shift into reverse and find a behavior that's the *opposite* of what is stated in the affirmation, rather than following the more direct route of simply doing as it is told. For example, "I don't want to be sick any longer" is not the same clear directive as *"I am focused on being healthy."*

Positively phrased affirmations also leave less room for doubt about what we want. They represent the difference between saying "I'll try to meet you if I can possibly make it" and "I will be there." We say, *"This* is what I want" rather than "Well, I'm not sure what I really want, but I know I don't want *that."*

### HOW TO CREATE POWERFUL AFFIRMATIONS

The best affirmations are those that captivate your imagination. They arise from the true desires you have discovered through your intuitive sensing and different forms of visualizations. They are:

**Worded in the first person, present tense.** Using the first-person "I" makes affirmations our own. And even when we're not experiencing a great sense of well-being at the moment, we need to word affirmations in the present tense. Examples:

• "I am a happy and secure person." (*Not* "I *will be* a happy and secure person." or "It's good to be happy and secure.")

• "I am ready for the perfect relationship." (*Not* "I will be ready for the perfect relationship when it comes along." or "It would be great to have a perfect relationship.")

**Backed by positive feelings and emotions.** If you are affirming that you are abundantly wealthy, or well-known for your creative talents, or in excellent health, use your imagination to experience exactly how you think that would feel to you. See your life as that of a very talented person, or as someone who is respected for their work, or who exudes health. See your surroundings under these circumstances and concentrate on the feelings you would have.

**Believed without question.** If you doubt what you are affirming, use it as an opportunity to discover and deflate that doubt. Then return to trusting and knowing that what you affirm is ideally true.

**Repeated regularly and often.** This can be done in a concentrated period of Mind Fitness exercising as you're walking, jogging, or driving, waiting in line, on hold, or for the microwave oven, or whenever you think of it in the course of a day.

**Stated clearly and positively.** Instead of "I will not eat any fattening foods today," try "Today I am choosing to eat only healthy, slimming foods." This is a clearer message to the mind, and concentrates on attaining a positive result rather than avoiding a negative one. It also eliminates the possibility that the mind might not catch that little "not" in the sentence and misinterpret—for example, "I will not smoke" as "I will smoke."

### *LIFE-AFFIRMING WORDS*

Even when we are not working on any specific issue, we can direct our energy into thoughts of good health and optimistic attitudes by focusing general statements of well-being. These sentences are self-directives reminding us of how we want to be.

### For Good Health
- I am strong, flexible, and healthy.
- I give thanks for being in good health.
- My body and I are friends and I want to take care of it.
- I relax my body and mind by taking a deep breath.
- I choose healthy things to optimize my health.

### For Emotional Well-Being
- I remain centered and calm.
- I am relaxed and at ease.

- I value being a humorous person.
- I respond to others with loving compassion.
- My emotions are wonderful guides for me.
- I keep my positive feelings out front as much as possible.

## For the Intellect
- I am open to new things.
- I grasp new information easily and respond appropriately.
- I welcome the higher wisdom that flows into me.
- I am flexible and creative in my thinking.
- I have unexpected creative thoughts that are strokes of genius.
- The most amazingly profitable thoughts come into my mind.

## For Spiritual Growth
- I am one with others. I know and embrace that part of me that is larger than any personality or physical form.
- I am part of the expanding life force, the highest good of which I can conceive.
- I am a trusting, loved, and loving person. I feel peaceful in myself. I smile to myself in gratitude.
- I am comforted as I join with others who share this earth with me. I affirm my human family.
- I feel the gentleness of Divine love sweep through me.

### SHAPING REALITY

**Words carry power.** This is an important theme that runs through Mind Fitness. When we consciously engage our minds in repeating affirmations, we take charge of what our mind is saying to our body. The process of affirming brings all the parts of us together—mind, body, brain, heart, and spirit—and lets them function as an integrated whole. This is a tremendously empowering process

We are learning that our beliefs create what we think of as reality, and that we only perceive those things in which we believe. It is very difficult for us to see something that we cannot think of as real, even if it is right in front of us. If we saw a unicorn on the way to work, our first thought would probably *not* be, "Gee, and all this time I've thought that unicorns didn't exist! I must have been wrong." Our first thought would probably be that someone was trying to trick us by attaching a fake horn to a small horse, or that we must be seeing things.

So we perceive what we can believe in, or what we *expect* to perceive—the things that are in our "belief set." Consciously choosing which affirmations we want to repeat to ourselves is one way of expanding our belief sets to include more *successful perceptions of ourselves and our situation.*

If we repeat six times a day for a month, "People want to support me. No one is out to get me. Most people only want to do things that will help me," this may very well alter and shape our reality, our perception of the way people relate to us. The synapses will be changed, the way we think about ourselves will be expanded, and the way we think about and respond to other people will be transformed.

One of our seminar participants wanted to think more positively about what she *did* have in her life, rather than always dwelling on what she *didn't* have in her life and how unhappy she was. She decided on the affirmation "I have everything I need to be happy now."

After a month, she came back to the group to report that something amazing had happened. On the fifth day of guiding her thinking with this affirmation, she began to notice things that had been in her life all along, but that she had never perceived as contributing to her happiness. She began to appreciate the wonderful house she lived in, and her cat's affection, and all the friends she had. Not only did she realize that she was much happier than she'd thought, but it actually seemed to her that more positive things and people came into her life each day.

She began to think of affirmations as magnets, and that is exactly how they work.

# Chapter 10

## RHYTHM AND STYLE

There is another element to Mind Fitness that is just as important as relaxation, visualization, and affirmation. It is rhythm and style—that is, being in harmony with the styles or rhythms inherent in the various activities we undertake, and with our own personal rhythms and styles.

### PERSONAL RHYTHM

We all have our own individual patterns of energy, and styles of learning and operating in the world. Some of us are more outgoing, assertive, and independent; others are more internal, calm, and collaborative. Some of us are auditory; others are visual or tactile learners. Some of us are morning people; others are night people. Some like to move in and assess a situation immediately; others like to "wait and see." Some need to nap in the afternoon; others require only a few hours of sleep each night. Some of us like a faster pace in life, and others a slower one.

We all have a sense of our internal patterns. It's important to accept and embrace those patterns, and incorporate them into a personalized program of Mind Fitness.

If you are a morning person, for example, and fade fast after 7:00 p.m., you would not want to schedule your inner-mind focusing time for 11:00 p.m. If you're a night person and don't really come alive until noon, you probably don't want to make your Mind Fitness time 6:00 a.m. The key is to find the time when it's easiest for you to be both relaxed and alert, so that you can bring your best to your Mind Fitness session.

We want to create our own rhythms within our Mind Fitness program, by using repetitive associations to help us move more quickly and easily into the states of relaxation, inner listening, imaging, and affirming. We can put reinforcement principles to work for us, using certain sounds, smells, and sights to help trigger our inner rhythms.

Some of us reflect best in front of a small altar with incense, candles, and soft music. Others may prefer sitting by the ocean, or in the garden, or on the sofa in the living room. We each have our own favorite kinds of music. It's not important what our personal rhythms *are*, just that we become aware of them and use them to our advantage, rather than trying to work against them because they don't "look right" or we have never done it that way before.

## *ACTIVITY RHYTHM*

This is pretty obvious, but it's amazing how often it's overlooked. Each individual activity also has its own inherent natural rhythm. The rhythm of golf is different from the rhythm of basketball. The rhythm and style of a household project is different from the rhythm and style needed for a business venture. As we do visualizations and affirmations that relate to improving our health or performance in various activities, we need to be conscious of the activity's own built-in rhythm and use it to our advantage.

It's easy to grow discouraged by thinking something will happen sooner than it will. For example, the rhythm of healing from major surgery is very different from that of getting over the flu. If you know the rhythm of healing from the surgery, you are not apt to grow frustrated by the longer time needed for complete recovery. You are expecting it to take longer, and indeed it does. The important thing is that you have consciously considered the rhythm of the activity and doesn't expect it to be different from what it is. If you go to a doctor appointment expecting it to take 15 minutes, you are probably going to experience frustration and stress. (When was the last time anyone went to a doctor and was in and out in 15 minutes?) Being realistic in your assessments of your activity's rhythm cycles and needs is really important to your mental health and peace of mind.

### WORKING WITH YOUR RHYTHM

Each of us knows how we learn best, and what kind of environment will help us most as we begin our Mind Fitness program. We may respond to visual elements, and have candles or flowers in the place where we do our Mind Fitness exercises. We may use a scent such as perfume or flowers to trigger mental patterns that put us into the state we want for this relaxing time. We may respond strongly to sounds, and want to play the same music each day so that our bodies and minds get used to that rhythm as part of our visualizing and affirming process. I suggest playing the same piece of quiet music to yourself during your sessions to help trigger your relaxation responses.

Whatever rhythms we use, the point is to start establishing our "grooves" so that when we hear that music, smell that fragrance, or see that candle, we go more quickly and easily into the open and relaxed state we are seeking. It boils down to this: The Mind Fitness session is a daily time that involves relaxing the body and mind, and shifting our attention from the outside world inward to where we shape our reality. These few minutes of quieting for proactive reflection and purposeful imagery *do* actually shape our reality. They guide our perceptions and expand what we are open to experiencing.

Now that we have covered the basic components of Mind Fitness, let's look at the seven steps recommended for a concentrated and empowered mind.

's

# Chapter 11

# *A DAILY WORKOUT*

*Doing Mind Fitness creates an orientation toward full potential and health in your life.* It is really saying "yes" to our own well-being, knowing that our well-being leads to better decisions and actions in the outer world.

The core steps in any Mind Fitness program can be done in a simple seven-step workout that usually takes about twenty minutes. Ideally, you'll do it every day at the same time, in the same place, although you can do it anytime and anywhere. I personally *have* to do it "anytime, anywhere"— but I do make sure I focus inward each and every day in some place and in some way. This may be closing my eyes at the airport, or sitting quietly in my car for fifteen to twenty minutes, or closing my eyes for a few breaths before an appointment.

But I make sure I do this every day, and that is the secret. You will personalize your program, tailoring it to fit your own rhythms and goals, but the seven steps described in this chapter will still form the ideal foundation—a backbone, if you will—for creating increased peace and health in your life.

Just as with physical fitness, each person's Mind Fitness workout program is unique. I want to emphasize this: *Each person's approach to their own well-being will be different from anyone else's.* So feel free to experiment with your own approach to your own time-out session. Experiment with various techniques, be creative, and above all, make sure your Mind Fitness workout is rejuvenating, peaceful, and empowering for you.

### FINDING YOUR RHYTHM

Some people like a longer relaxation period, and take extra time to enjoy that peaceful, serene place within themselves; others relax more quickly and go immediately to their visualizations and affirmations. Some people like a very dramatic setting with altar, flowers, incense, and music; others prefer a more low-key session, and are content just to sit quietly on the sofa and journey inward. Some people see their Mind Fitness workout as the most dynamic and creative period of their day; others see it as the most restful time.

The important thing is to choose the mental and physical environment and rhythms that work best for you. Choose the surroundings that make you feel most at home and most comfortable. As you start doing the program every day, you will begin to know what those are. All that's necessary is that you be able to sit comfortably in a chair or on the floor.

When you can, work on sitting up straight so that energy can flow all through your body. Sitting up is preferable to lying down—so that you remain alert and relaxed rather than falling asleep—but I do sometimes lie down to do my quieting. There are no rules—just get to know what is peaceful for you. Make the commitment to being quiet with yourself each day. Even if all you do is sit down quietly and take five very slow, conscious deep breaths, you will feel the healing begin.

Remember these keys to success:

1.  Set aside time each day for relaxing, visualizing, and affirming.
2.  Do your exercises as regularly as possible, preferably at the same time each day.

3. When possible, create a special place that allows you to remember the greater whole in your life.

If Mind Fitness is so simple, why does it take practice? Why can't we just toss off a ten to twenty-minute session every week or two, and get the same results?

There are three reasons.

First, personal negativity patterns are usually lifelong habits. We have twenty, forty, sixty, or more years of negative training of habits to overcome. It's as if we have spent all those years looking for love in all the wrong places. It takes some doing to break those old habits. We're involved in a process of stopping the momentum in one direction, and actively fueling it in another.

Without a regular program of mental reflection and focus that actively steers the mind away from negativity and replaces it with something positive, we tend to gravitate back toward our old, familiar patterns of thinking. Left to our own devices, we will more often see the limited and difficult side of things.

Second, part of our negative programming—if we are focused on feelings of defeat—may be that we don't *deserve* to have a new, positive perspective and all the benefits that it brings. We may be able to visualize the ideal life, job, or relationship, but somewhere in our unconscious, we don't believe that we are entitled to it or are capable of achieving it.

We may even go so far as to sabotage ourselves with self-defeating, negative mind-chatter, like "That would be nice, but what have I ever done to deserve it? Even if I got it, I'd just mess it up." or "That's a great job, but I could never get it."

We don't even have to put these thoughts into words for them to hold us back; we just have to let them fester somewhere within our general attitudinal atmosphere.

Third, making the move from generalized negativity to optimistic health means not just breaking old habits, but actively establishing new ones. It takes time to establish new patterns of thought, and having something specific to do each day—such as the twenty-minute Mind Fitness session with its seven specific steps—is a good way to make that new habit stick.

As we all know, developing new habits takes time and attention, especially at first. It takes effort to develop the habit of sitting down each day and quietly focusing yourself, but it is usually easier than you expect. Once you make the time and get started, it's really enjoyable to relax and imagine your possibilities. If you aren't enjoying your images, change them so that you *are*! Be sure you're having fun with your Mind Fitness. You are really engaging in mental play—creating things in your mind exactly the way you would ideally like to see them in your own personality and in your daily activities.

Starting your own program is a wonderful commitment to yourself. It begins the healing process and begins to build a new base for relating both to ourselves and to others. We are creating a new filter through which to see these things, a positive filter that makes everything in life fuller and more joyous. We are moving into a fuller flow in life, and we are going to find that everything is easier because we are more accepting and positive.

### THE SEVEN-STEP PROGRAM

The first step in this exercise—the one we have to do even before the step listed as #1—is to *suspend judgment*. If we are used to resisting and reacting negatively to new things, there will be a temptation to say things like:

- "This will never work for me."
- "This is stupid . . . just a bunch of Pollyanna stuff."
- "I don't believe in this. It's just another 'positive thinking' trick."

- "It might work for other people, but I won't be able to do it right."

Just for now, try to give up any opinions, decisions, judgments, or second-guessing, and follow the seven steps. This can be really hard for people who are quick to judge and put down most things in life. We can begin to sabotage ourselves even before we begin . . . or we can take a more courageous attitude and actually start the healing before we start the seven steps. It's our choice.

*Step 1: Stretching*

Relaxing the body is the first step to relaxing the mind, and stretching is one of the best ways to release tension and bring oxygen into your body. Take a minute to stretch your body and release any tightness in your joints or muscles. Any easy stretches will do; here are some ideas:

- **Tiptoes:** Stand on your tiptoes and gently reach your hands and arms over your head. Stretch as if you are trying to reach the ceiling (or the stars). Hold this position for a moment and then lower your arms.
- **Shoulder Circles:** Bring your shoulders up to your ears and lower them as you rotate your shoulder blades in circles. Shoulders have been called the "should do's"—we often use them to "carry our burdens." As you move and stretch your shoulders, imagine those "burdened" attitudes releasing and drifting out of your body, into the air.
- **The Turtle:** This ancient Chinese stretch is very good for the nervous system. Lower your chin to your chest, feeling your spine lengthen as you breathe in. Then raise your chin and squeeze your shoulders up to your ears as you exhale. Lower your shoulders to normal position and feel the decrease in tension. End by tilting your head from side to side, ear toward shoulder, to gently stretch your neck.

- **Arm Swinging:** Standing with your feet two to three feet apart, extend your arms out from the shoulders and swivel to the left, then the right. Swing way around so that you see behind you. Do this circular movement about ten times to release tension from the spine and put energy back into the hands. Be sure to stretch your face at the same time by smiling and releasing any tension that's been held there.

- **The Cat:** The truly cat-like way to do this is to get down on your hands and knees on the floor (ideally, on the cushioning of a thick carpet or mat). Breathing in, stretch your spine and abdomen down toward the floor with your hips and shoulders moving upward. Then stretch the other way, rounding your lower back slowly up toward the ceiling. You can also do this standing, by moving your lower back and your shoulders in opposite directions, slowly arching your spine forward and backward.

I do all these exercises to shake off built-up tensions before sitting down. You may do them all, choose those that work best for you, or do other stretches that you like and find relaxing. These stretches take perhaps sixty seconds and make it much easier to relax mentally and emotionally once you sit down. They help us leave behind the physical tensions of stress and living, preparing us for the mental stretching to come.

*Step 2: Preparing*

Do yourself the favor of unplugging your phone or switching off the ring. Do everything you can to eliminate intrusions and distractions. Some people keep a journal handy to note down any insights they may get. Now sit down, either cross-legged on the floor or a cushion, or in a comfortable chair, with posture erect and feet on the floor. As mentioned before, lying down may make you sleepy, since the alpha brain-wave state reached in relaxation is close to the edge of sleep. Sitting up makes it easier to achieve a relaxed but alert and wakeful state.

The value of having a particular place for your practice is that you begin to form a positive habit. Each time you sit in that place, draw a few deep breaths, and go through your relaxation, visualization, and affirmation exercises, the habit becomes stronger. It gets easier to reach and maintain that state of relaxation. You move more easily through your visualizations and affirmations.

Whatever place you've chosen, take a few moments to make it yours and settle in. Just simply sit in that comfortable chair for a few minutes and tell yourself that this is your time, the most important part of your day.

*Step 3: Relaxation*

This is the time when you become a human *being* rather than a human *doing*. Try playing a relaxation meditation tape (you can make a tape of the relaxation meditation at the end of chapter 7, or use one of the excellent tapes that are available commercially), or simply go through a meditation yourself, silently or aloud.

Relaxation is like preparing the soil for planting the seeds of your own growth and health. Think of this as the time to remove any large rocks from your garden and to prepare the rows for planting.

Close your eyes. Slowly focus on your breathing and the quiet warmth of relaxation moving though your body. Consciously release any tensions as you become aware of them. Move through your body, relaxing toes and arches of the feet, calves, thighs, buttocks, abdomen, chest, shoulders, arms, hands, jaw, face and skull. Replace any tightness with warmth and quiet.

Breathe full, deep breaths into your abdominal area. Focus on your breathing, perhaps even counting your breaths. Allow a sense of quietness to come over you. Tell yourself that for the next few minutes you are giving yourself permission to completely relax your body and your mind.

Go over your meditation for relaxation—bring to mind the pond image or another relaxation exercise you like—and tell yourself in words that you are now experiencing what it feels like to be completely at peace, in harmony with yourself and the world. As you get to know how this state feels, it will be easier to maintain it at other times during your day. Remember you are teaching yourself something new—a skill that can be used in many different situations—and there is no right or wrong way to do it.

### Step 4: Intuitive Listening

Now that we have relaxed physically and mentally, we want to turn more inward. This is the time during the Mind Fitness sessions to simply sit quietly and listen. Listening inward is an active process. You listen to your heart beating within your body, and then to your breath as it enters and leaves your lungs. Listen to your own mind, its restlessness and its moments of quiet. Through this listening, we can become aware of a deeper, quieter, wiser part of us. That is the soul level of intuition.

For many of us, so much "doing nothing" may be hard at first. Your mind may be restless and flighty as it moves from one "essential" thought to another. That's fine. Think of this as just a time each day to shift your attention from the outer world to your inner world, and let the process take its own shape. You are simply allowing the quiet to form within you as you open yourself up to any images, urges, flashes of intuition, insight, or natural knowing that may come to you. We have all had those moments of insight in which there is a major shift in our thinking. It may be a new understanding that allows for forgiveness, or an insight that causes us to change our direction rather radically. You are now proactively guiding yourself to a mental quieting level at which you are more likely to experience those moments of insight and intuitive understandings.

If nothing comes to you, simply relax and enjoy the quiet time with no pressures about what you "should do" or " ought to be." New research tells us that you are doing exactly what is best for your overall health and well-being: Taking time to relax and de-stress. Balancing your body and mind. Allowing your mind and body to rid themselves of tension. Maybe this is the "cleansing ritual" for the mind and muscles—think of it as soaking your mind in a nice hot bath for twenty minutes. Any way you want to look at it, you are doing exactly what you should be doing for optimal health and well-being.

The intuition, with its symbols, is a gateway to the inner unconscious, source of our most powerful thoughts and urges. The intuition speaks softly but persistently. It does not scream or obsess: that is the ego's role. In most of daily life, the ego's demands drown out the intuition's whispers. But when we sit quietly, relax, and turn our awareness inward, we can more readily receive feelings and insights from our intuition.

The inner voice isn't just some ephemeral, passive, fleeting sense. It is the conduit through which we translate our true desires and inner strengths into goals and action in the world. We may think of it as our true nature, our essence, the True part of us. It is from this True part that we come to understand what we really want in our lives, so that we focus our attention and skills in that direction. Many people spend a lifetime pursuing goals that actually don't mean much to them. When we listen to the inner voice, we tend to hear a truer part that allows us to express ourselves more honestly and authentically in the world. We are carried forward by a fuller, purer energy, because the dreams and goals are really ours.

*Step 5: Visualization*

Now that you are completely relaxed and at peace within yourself, and have opened up to the intuitive self, it's time for a few minutes of visualizing. This is the proactive part of reflecting: You actively use the mind to mentally experience images of how you ideally want to experience different things in your life. You use the focused imagination to experience the possibilities, the ideal—rather than just seeing the all-too-obvious problems within different areas and relationships in your life. You direct the mental movies from your ideal viewpoint, so you can begin to focus in that direction in daily life.

Note: Before you begin your Mind Fitness sessions, you may want to plan what you want to focus on, so you'll have in mind some visual images to start with. This is especially true if you are focusing, over a longer period of time, on a particular life issue such as health or a relationship. You don't *have* to plan ahead; it's fine to just discover what naturally comes to mind from the intuitive mind. Sometimes the most unexpected thoughts and insights pop up in the quiet. We'll talk in the next chapter about choosing what you want to work on, and selecting powerful images and visualizations for that particular goal.

For now, let's take examples of two kinds of life goals— one specific, and one more general—and see how you might go about visualizing for each of them. Of course, the more specific you can get about your goals, the easier they will be to work on. But sometimes we just aren't ready to get specific. It may take some time to work down from "Feeling better about myself" to "Being more positive at work" to "Not letting my boss, Ed, get to me when he asks me to work overtime."

**Specific Goal Story:** Joan's youngest child started college last fall and she found herself rattling around the house, getting more bored and irritable by the day. While the kids were growing up she had worked part-time, a year here and a year there, but had never found anything she particularly liked and never felt that she could put much energy into any of her jobs. They were really just ways to bring in a little extra money and keep herself from going stir-crazy.

But now she was starting a whole new life and wanted a career to which she could devote the energy she'd given to the kids. The problem was, she saw and labeled herself as "just a housewife" with few skills and no competitive edge. She had thought about getting a job in public relations or real estate, but knew she didn't have those skills and lacked the confidence to think she could learn them.

After a few sessions focusing on her strengths and desires, Joan was able to see that she wasn't completely unskilled, and that in fact she had tremendous organizational ability. She could walk into any house, or any office, and set things up so that they worked. She was also able to see that this was a skill she could put to use in either public relations or real estate as an office manager.

Still, she had her doubts. She hadn't had a full-time job since she'd gotten married twenty years earlier, and wasn't sure anyone would want to hire her.

When Joan came to the visualization part of her Mind Fitness workout, she let herself flow into an image of herself in an office—moving around with confidence, enjoying the respect of the people around her, making a contribution to what they were doing, and feeling the satisfaction that came from doing a good job.

She pictured what she was wearing, and how it felt to sit at her desk and work with the various files, and talk with people who came by her desk. She took herself through the whole day, from arriving in the morning and taking off her coat, through the morning and lunchtime to the afternoon, and finally to leaving in the evening.

She saw the things she did, and more importantly, she let herself realistically imagine the actual experience of going through that day. She felt the emotions, tasted the coffee, heard the various office sounds, saw the people moving around, and imagined everything as it would be if it were perfect.

After a week of visualizing this scene every day in increasing detail, Joan was ready to make some calls and start interviewing. She had spent the necessary time to really sequence through what would be asked of her and how she would feel about doing each of the tasks. She had slowed herself down enough to combine her left-brain sequencing and analyzing skills and her right-brain sensing and imaging skills to "try on" this experience in her mind.

The experience of successfully managing an office was real to her. She knew she could do it, and that they'd be lucky to have her.

It's often said that the unconscious does not distinguish between an experience that is imagined, and one that actually happens. Joan was wise to pump images of confidence and remind her unconscious how competent she was, before she had to go out and convince a prospective boss.

**General Direction Story:** Ben was so low that all he could come up with as a goal for visualization was to not feel so terrible when he got up in the morning. He wasn't ill or hung over, he just had no energy and no desire to get out of bed. For now, it wasn't even important for Ben to discover *why* he felt so awful; he just needed some relief.

The first thing Ben had to do was switch around his goal from "not feeling so terrible" to "feeling like something is worthwhile getting out of bed for." Visualizations, affirmations, and goals always work better when they are stated positively. Then he had to decide what it would feel like to feel good when he got up in the morning.

Ben's visualization was simple. He came into his state of

relaxation, listened to the inner voice, and then began to see himself in bed before he woke up in the morning. He saw himself sleeping peacefully, and then beginning to stir. As he began to wake up, Ben actually became the man in the bed and imagined himself slowly coming to consciousness and becoming aware of the things around him. He saw the clock on his bedside table and the morning light starting to come through his bedroom curtain. He smelled the coffee in the kitchen downstairs and felt the soft, cool sheets against his arms.

He focused this thinking. He thought about seeing a bird fly against the blue sky and really visualized that bird until a smile started to spread across his face, and he began to get into that experience. Ben loved birds, so he used that image as "something that is worth getting out of bed for." He consciously thought about other nice things he could do that day, and the ways he could make that particular Tuesday more pleasant for himself.

Ben had to be a little bit of an actor. At first he had to pretend to be more positive than he actually felt in the mornings. "Fake it and you'll make it" became his motto. Over the course of a month, it became easier and easier for Ben to walk himself through this visualization. Soon he didn't have to fake it any more; he moved through the visualization smoothly and effortlessly. He began to enjoy it so much, in fact, that he started doing the same visualization just as he actually woke up every morning. It wasn't long before he was actually living his images and even surprised himself by jumping out of bed enthusiastically one morning.

In the next chapter, we will discuss more visualizations for healing and mastery. You will want to create your personal images to suit your own wants and needs, and on some days you may just want to do some general visualizations for personal healing and expanding different aspects of yourself.

You might simply form an image of the kind of person

you want to be, and focus on one or two aspects of that change during your visualization. If you try to focus on too many things, your energy may get scattered and the visualization won't be as effective. Remember that when you heal one aspect of yourself, you affect all aspects of yourself. See, feel, hear, and experience yourself responding to someone who has been a problem for you. See yourself handling the situation as you would want to handle it. See, feel, and experience yourself getting out of bed in the morning with exactly the kind of attitude you would like to have. See, feel, and experience yourself moving through your day, taking care of your daily tasks with lightness and a sense of humor. Give yourself a road map of how you would ideally like to feel and be.

If any negative behaviors slip into your visualization, see yourself stopping, realizing what you are doing, and changing that behavior. Experience a sense of love for yourself for taking the time and effort to release your limiting attitudes. You are teaching yourself new, more personally validating ways of thinking. Fill your visualizations with details and feelings. Make them as vivid and real as you can. Know that you become what you image.

### Step 6: Affirmation

Affirmations work directly with visualizations. They are directed words of intention and direction that we give ourselves in order to help us stay on track. Affirmations are statements that take the intuitive images, deeper understandings, and insights, and translate them so that they make sense to the language-oriented human brain. Affirmations integrate imagery with verbal words.

Affirmations are also the emotionally felt "*I can!*" part of the visualization, the statement to our rational mind that the things we visualize are actually possible for us. Words give us clear directions. Positive words direct us to stop automatic mental chatter that can play continually and automatically in our minds.

It's best to begin your affirmations while you are actually doing your imaging. While you are still visualizing, start to talk to yourself in a directed and purposeful way, using the statements of affirmation you have chosen. Give yourself a positive script to create these mental movies. For example, Joan, the housewife seeking work as an office manager, might use some of these affirmations:

- "I am a competent person who contributes to any group or set of circumstances" while she sees herself interacting within a group of imaged coworkers.
- "I am capable and particularly gifted with an ability to organize things" while she imagines herself organizing people and workloads.
- "When I interview for jobs, people sense my abilities and want to hire me" as she envisions herself sitting in an office during an interview.

Ben might tell himself:

- "The first things I experience in the morning—the sheets, the smell of coffee, the sound of birds, the morning light— are all joys to me. I am eager to get up and start doing something positive" while seeing himself doing exactly that.
- "I am enthusiastic about each day. I know why I am here and what I am doing" while mentally rehearsing himself looking out at the sunshine and feeling good.
- "Cut the self-indulgent whining! I can look forward to getting involved in my life and others' in a positive way" as he imagines himself cutting a ribbon of whine and seeing a few of his good fortunes, such as his wife, home, and health.

**Verbal Clear Directions:** You will find that just the right words of direction will surface from your intuition. Don't be afraid to try several different statements and words until you sense the one that is most powerful for you. These short, positive phrases help keep the mind on track. We're in the process of replacing long-standing habits of mind, so we'll need to re-peat to ourselves the clarifying statement of intention, the affirmation, in order to get our minds going in the new direction. You know how easy it is to slip back into a habit. These statements help stop the automatic negative habit and set you on the path of clear direction.

You may want to print your intentions on cards and leave them various places in your home—on mirrors, on the refrig-erator, by your desk. It helps to add a little drawing, or a visual symbol like a circle or square that will remind you of your intention to move on with your life. Goals are easier to remember when paired with a picture. As you hold these words in your mind, know that they have the power of your dreams behind them; they are clear, concise self-direction with no doubt that you can create them in your own life.

*Step 7: Finishing*

This is the completion of your workout, a time to come back from your quiet world into the outer world. Wiggle your fin-gers and toes, open your eyes, and stretch your arms out wide.

Congratulate and acknowledge yourself for having de-voted this time and energy to your growth, happiness, and well-being. Know that you face the world with more resources and balance now than you did twenty minutes ago.

Remind yourself that attitudinal health improvement doesn't take place *only* in these quiet times. It becomes more a part of your life all the time, every day. You don't have to be sitting down with your eyes closed in order to "pump images" as bodybuilders pump iron. You'll have many opportunities each day to give yourself some quick affirmations, and briefly flash a visual image of an event that you want to happen, or simply flood yourself with the experience of being the person you want to be. You can do these things while walking down the street, driving the car, doing the dishes, even typing or doing other activities that may not require 100 percent of your attention.

You may need to give your new and positive attitudes a great deal of attention at first. They are like infants in the beginning—unsteady and a little fragile. You need to build them up and make them strong, so that they can carry you rather than your carrying them. That is the transition you're looking for, and it comes with perseverance.

The first few times you go through your Mind Fitness workout, you may feel a little awkward or uncomfortable. You may have to stop and check on the steps at first. That's the newness of it all combined with your normal resistance to quieting and perhaps even to changing yourself. Remember that this will pass. Everything will start to get much easier very quickly. You will start to feel more in charge, and more creative. You will begin to see the results, and then the process of health and empowerment really gets exciting. When you begin to have the confidence that comes from success, your Mind Fitness work become very powerful.

Practicing consistently, each day, restructures the inner voice—from old, destructive habits into new, life-affirming patterns of thinking. We begin to experience changes in our lives and, more importantly, in the way we feel about ourselves and relate to others. Ideally, each day becomes a treasure, rather than something we have to get through. We begin living joyfully and creatively, no matter what our daily activities are. We begin to feel a light within us—the kind of active love that doesn't just wait for things to happen, but makes the most of each day. An inner peace and calm emerges.

Now, let's explore some of the visualizations that people have found particularly useful.

# PART THREE

## BUILDING STEADY ATTITUDES

# Chapter 12

## *IMAGES AND TECHNIQUES: POSITIVE MOMENTUM*

We have an infinite number and variety of images at our disposal. The mind is limitless, and can come up with constructive images for most situations or conditions if we let it.

As we get into the new habit of forming images of love, goal fulfillment, and generosity, something very powerful happens in our lives. The basic energy behind everything we do begins to change, to become unlocked, moving with more synergy. We begin to feel more positive and connected as we come to feel that we are in charge of our lives—at least on the inside—and have the desire and willingness to succeed and be happy. The filter through which we look at life becomes more giving, more optimistic, and more enthusiastic. We have a developing self-belief that things are going to work out for the highest good even if we can't see it right now.

Once this process begins, it starts to feed on itself and snowball. One success breeds another. One loving thought or moment makes the next one easier. One act of kindness to ourselves and others grows into two or three. *We begin to build a positive momentum.*

In time we become more skilled at developing our own

personal images of self-direction, healing, and mastery. They begin to bubble to the surface without effort, because we are in closer contact with our inner voices and have more access to the power of the unconscious. Healthful images become available to us more automatically, replacing the old familiar habits of judgment and negativity.

But sometimes, before becoming masters of directed inner seeing or visualization, we need a jump start. The following visualizations are ones I've used with good results, and ones that other people recommended to me as being successful in their lives. Some are general, and some specific. As you read through them, find and use those that resonate with you. Perhaps some of them will prompt other ideas that relate specifically to your issues.

As you develop your own images, remember to concentrate on your own rhythms. If you are a person who likes experiencing things through sound, make sound or music a part of your images. If you like touching, make that an important part of your images. Let yourself gravitate to the things you most enjoy, and use them to enhance your visualizations. Make each a strong sensual experience, one that captivates you while you are in it.

Remember to draw on images and sensory experiences that have deep and rich experiential meaning *for you*. You can mentally place yourself on a beach or a mountain, in a forest, skiing, sailing, or simply reading quietly by a fire. The particulars of the scene aren't as important as the fact that they have *personal meaning* for you and can bring forth deep *feelings*.

### MODEL VISUALIZATIONS

These template or model visualizations are more than jump starts for your own personal images. They are wonderful tools to develop and keep available for when you need some quick help. When you find yourself succumbing to a negative spin on the situation at hand, having an already familiar visualization handy can help you lift yourself out of it at a moment's notice.

When everything gets to you at the same time—kids, boss, workload, even the weather—it's not realistic to expect yourself to sit down then and there and come up with a new, creative visualization designed just for those circumstances. In the middle of a bout with negativity and defeatism, those images aren't always right at our fingertips. By thinking ahead and preparing some images for emergencies, we can keep ourselves centered and calm in the midst of chaos. We need these visualizations quickly retrievable on demand, as available to us as phone numbers or the words to a song we love.

The power of template visualizations is that they are repeated often. We have already established the "grooves" in our mind that bring them into our experience and let us reap the benefits.

As you slowly read these visualizations, concentrate on seeing the images and feeling the sensations. Think of some others that might be particularly meaningful to you.

### EMPTYING YOUR MENTAL CLOSET

*I walk into the mental closet of my mind. I start to notice all the dark, ill-fitting clothes that are scattered around the closet. Some are hanging off hangers, others are balled up on the floor, some are doubled up on each other. I take a deep breath and start to throw out all the no longer desirable items. I start to really clean house, as they say. And each time I toss something away I say "good-bye, xxxxxxx," naming whatever negative characteristic I want to name. As I discard each old dark piece of clothing that I no longer want or need, I feel a lightness and a quiet joy within me. Finally I am doing what I have wanted to do for ages. Yes, it feels wonderful to finally clean out the closet of unwanted habits and tendencies.*

## VISUALIZATION FOR PEACE

*I am seated in a lush garden with gentle hills and berry bushes all around. The flowers are bursting with brilliant purple, red, and yellow blossoms and I can feel a breeze on my sun-warmed face and arms. I get up and walk slowly around the garden, staying on the white stone pathway. I slowly move through the colorful flowers, stopping to smell the red ones, and touching the petals of the blue blossoms. I feel a sense of complete harmony and tranquility fill my entire body and mind. I take a deep breath and know that I am safe and at peace. With each breath, I feel a deeper level of peace fall over me, touching my body, my mind, and even my soul. The sweet gentle air brings with each breath a renewed depth of serenity and harmony.*

This visualization works great in times when you want to fill yourself with quiet, either because of a stressful situation or because you are now ready to really sit down and relax in a deep way. The more you use it, the more quickly you'll reach a state of relaxation and peacefulness. Remember, the effects are cumulative.

## VISUALIZATION FOR ENERGY

I have two favorite visualizations for energy:

**1. Shaft of Light.** *I walk up to a brightly sparkling shaft of light and stand gazing into it. As I look into the shaft of sparkling light, I take in a deep breath and let go of all my tensions, both physical and mental. When I am ready, I lift my arms up over my head as if doing a giant stretch, and walk into the center of the shaft of light.*

*I take the light into my body through my breath and all my pores, allowing it to fill me with a high and powerful energy. I concentrate on feeling the tingling in each of my cells and in my limbs. When I am filled with energizing light, I simply open my eyes and affirm that this energy is now within me and I am ready for whatever is next.*

**2. Spring Board:** *I stand on a giant springboard and begin to jump up and down, filled with delight and fun. Each time, I jump higher and higher with my arms swinging, and each time I jump, I feel myself filled with more energy to accomplish whatever I want.*

This is a visualization to "pump yourself up" and give yourself an extra burst of energy when you need it. It is particularly effective for people who learn best through movement.

### THE DOORWAY VISUALIZATION

*I begin by taking several deep breaths and see in front of me a doorway. Sometimes it is large and impressive; other times, it is simple and natural. It can be studded with jewels, or made of simple bamboo; high and arching or low and cozy. And the doorway can be different each time I approach it, depending on how I feel.*

*Slowly, the door swings open. On the other side are health, creativity, love, healing, compassion, happiness, peacefulness, and everything I've ever wanted in life. It's there waiting for me; all I have to do is walk through the door.*

*I take another deep breath, step across the threshold, and enter the world of my dreams. I pause for a moment to look around and see exactly what is here. What work am I doing? Who are the people in my life? How do I relate to them? What do I feel like? Can I let myself have all this good? As I breathe in one final time, I know that all of this is within me and I accept it with a smile.*

### INTENTIONAL RELIVING

Intentionally reliving certain events or experiences in the mind's eye so that they are the way we want them to be is one of the most valuable tools of Mind Fitness, and one of the most powerful ways to use visualization. It constructively joins imagination with logical and imagery skills and can be *a key element in healing*. Mental rehearsal from the point of view of our ideal holds a lot of teaching and directing value for us. It is a way of actually replacing negative experiences with positive ones. We've said before that the unconscious can't distinguish between events that are imagined, and those that actually happen. Reliving events in a more positive vein begins to create new and *more positive* grooves in our mental patterns.

We can intentionally relive events in the past, in the present, and in the future. Reliving negative events from the past accomplishes two things: *healing* and *prevention*.

Not only does reliving events in a more positive way help to heal our thoughts and feelings about the event, it can actually help keep the problem from recurring. Understanding what actually happened, why it happened, and what we can do next time to prevent it is much more productive than beating ourselves up, feeling guilty, or blaming the other person.

**Intentional Reliving Story:** Every Saturday morning, Laura and her fourteen-year-old daughter Megan had a screaming battle about Megan cleaning her room. Over the last few months, Laura felt that this struggle had come to represent their entire relationship.

Megan was supposed to clean her room before she left the house each Saturday. But every Saturday, she came bounding down the stairs dressed to go out and almost made it to the front door before Laura yelled, "Megan, did you clean your room?"

There would be a sullen silence, and then one of an endless string of excuses: the football game, band practice, meeting a friend to study chemistry, or a sale at the department store. Laura was as infuriated by Megan's defiance as she was by the room not being clean, and the two of them launched into the regular Saturday morning screaming match.

When Laura started doing Mind Fitness, this was one of the first things she worked on. The fights with Megan on Saturday mornings left her drained and were beginning to set the tone for all their interactions.

Laura found some quiet time on Thursday afternoon and sat down in her own bedroom to do some intentional reliving. She played back what usually happened, looked to see what she was really feeling and what Megan might really be feeling, and then formed a picture in her mind of how she would like it to be.

The first thing she realized was that they weren't really fighting about Megan cleaning her room, but about the level of control that Laura had over Megan's life. Megan resented the fact that she was still "under Laura's thumb" and that her activities were restricted on a weekend day when her freedom was especially important to her. The more Megan resisted Laura's control, the greater became Laura's need to clamp down and *insist* on that control. It became a battle of wills—a test of who was in charge—that actually had very little to do with whether or not Megan's room was clean.

Laura closed her eyes and began to imagine the Saturday morning scene as she would like it to unfold next time. Instead of waiting for Megan to come bounding down the stairs as usual on Saturday morning, dressed to go out, Laura saw herself sitting down with Megan on Friday after school and having a talk.

She pictured both of them calm and connected with one another, willing to listen to one another's point of view. In her mind's eye, she saw herself working with Megan to come up with a solution to this problem of cleaning the room. Megan talked about how she hated having to do it on Saturday, and Laura asked her when she would like to do it. Laura didn't care *when* the room got cleaned, and had just chosen Saturday because that's when *she* had cleaned her room as a teen.

Megan said she wouldn't mind cleaning her room if she could do it on Thursday or Friday after school, and Laura thought that would be fine.

Both of them got what they wanted, and they didn't have to argue to make it happen. Having already gone through the entire scene in her imagination, Laura was ready to tackle the situation in "real life" and found that it unfolded almost exactly as it had in her imagination.

Intentional reliving can heal many kinds of hurts. It lets us *do* something about the questions:

- "How might I have handled that more graciously?"
- "What could I have done so that I felt better about that situation?"
- "How could we have avoided that fight?"
- "What might have allowed her to see my point of view, and let me get a better look at hers?"

Each time we relive an event in our imagination, we not only heal the past but create a positive program for the future.

## STOP, CANCEL, REPLACE

As we become more aware, we learn to react quickly, and can sometimes "relive" events *as they are happening* so that the negative attitudes and behaviors never have a chance to take root. When we notice ourselves starting down a negative or resistant path, we can:

- **STOP** the negative momentum by simply stopping whatever we are doing or thinking, and pause for a moment to acknowledge to ourselves that we are doing something that we no longer want to be doing; something that does not benefit us. We take a step to become self-directed; then we

- **CANCEL** the negative attitude or behavior. We just say "Cancel" and make a strong hand motion, like a chopping motion in the air, to anchor cancellation in our mind. Finally, we:
- **REPLACE** the negative attitude or behavior with what we *do* want to say or think. We replace what we no longer want to be doing with what is more supportive to us.

Obviously, we don't always have the time to sit down, close our eyes, light a candle, start the music, and take several deep breaths before we do this. In fact, sometimes our reactions have to be lightning-fast. If I find myself saying or thinking words that are from my old reactionary patterns, I just say "Cancel," make a chopping hand motion in the air to cut the energy, and then say it the new way. It takes only a moment.

**Rod's Story:** Rod thought that his father, Allan, had never gotten over Rod's decision to go to law school instead of trying for a career in pro football. Every time they talked on the phone, Allan steered the conversation around to football, commenting on various teams and noting how much money different players were making. He never wanted to hear about Rod's law practice, and fell silent when Rod brought up the subject.

As a result, nearly every time they spoke they had a fight. Rod couldn't stand not being acknowledged by his father, and Allan couldn't stand to consider the possibility that Rod had been right in not playing football.

Rod realized that he couldn't count on Allan's changing, and that if they were going to stop fighting, he had to be the one to do it. The triggers that prompted his negative outbursts were obvious; now he just had to find a way to stop himself in time.

Rod prepared by doing some intentional reliving during

his Mind Fitness workouts, imagining himself taking his father's backhanded criticism in stride. He focused on seeing his father with new understanding and loving forgiveness. Rod got clear on his position. He didn't want to become a doormat; neither did he want to feel that he had to defend himself and get into a fight with his father every time they talked. He decided he would take charge of how he was viewing things and give up wanting to change his father.

Sure enough, the next time Allan called, he started talking to Rod about the Bears game and how much money the new rookie was making. Rod's first instinct was to react and fight back, but instead, he took control of the situation. He told himself to STOP and CANCEL that negative pattern and replace it with understanding and love for his father. He let his father talk about the Bears and accepted him as he was. Later on, he was able to REPLACE it by changing the subject to something neutral.

It wasn't the last time Rod had to go through that conscious process, but this first success made the next one easier.

### MONSTERS

We all have certain primal fears. They usually originated in childhood, when we felt helpless and victimized, and sometimes they have tremendous power over us. If we know what they are, we can work on them in our personalized time-out sessions and strip them of their power. By anticipating what will happen the next time they pop up, and reliving the experience in advance, we can take control of more and more unconscious ground. We can do something about those monsters before they even come around.

**My Monster Story:** My monster found me when I was ten. He was the neighborhood bully, and my brother and I became the object of his daily scorn. I remember the feeling I always got when he was around. I felt terrified, resentful, and victimized. Feeling helpless and victimized led to anger and hatred, and I felt engulfed in the waves of despair and revengeful thoughts. Any form of abuse—physical or mental—terrorizes and leaves deep emotional wounds.

That particular day, I was walking down a quiet street. Suddenly I knew he was behind me; I could feel his presence. An overwhelming fear welled up inside me. When I walked faster, he walked faster. There was no place to hide, and I could feel his overpowering force beginning to swallow me up. As the moments ticked by, I felt as helpless as a mouse in a cage about to be consumed. He caught up with me and blocked my way. The solid blow to my stomach was so quick, so feared and shocking that to this day, I have that same bodily sensation whenever I feel overwhelmed.

When I began practice inner mind awareness I found a way to deal with the fear and anger that went back to this early incident. I focus on reliving in my imagination that experience with the bully, becoming aware of my body's tightening and constricting. I then replace that terror and anger by consciously focusing on relaxing my body with my breath and concentrating on feelings and scenes of safety. The idea is to feel the anger and pain, and then quickly replace those feelings with love, safety, and warmth. I focus on reprogramming my emotions by allowing myself to experience the old, negative ones, and then giving them an overlay of positive ones that begin to take away the bully's power.

I create a bridge from the negative to the positive, joining the two and quieting the old fear and anger with today's feelings of safety and love.

When those old "bully feelings" come up, I feel physical sensations in my body. When that happens, I quickly act to STOP, CANCEL, and REPLACE the old pattern with the new. It sounds mechanical, but knowing to do something mechanical when you're in trouble is very useful. Remember, you are not denying your feelings, but identifying and acknowledging them, then replacing the old feelings with new templates.

This technique can be used on other fearful symptoms. It's a matter of getting clear on what the triggers are, where those triggers come from, and the fact that we can do something about them.

## WATCHING FOR PITFALLS

We all have certain triggers that set off our own brand of darkness in us—certain people, places, and things that tend to rob us of our positive outlook and make us resistant, putting on the "gray-colored glasses." The trigger may be a visit to a particular relative, or being with certain friends who are inclined to be negative, or going out to certain restaurants or nightspots, or even the change of season from fall to winter.

It's important to be able to identify what these negativity triggers are, so that we can be on the lookout for them. The more aware we become of when we are likely to fall into negative thinking, the better able we are to avoid it. The blind person rarely stumbles on curbs because he makes a point of knowing where they are. In the same way, when we can identify the people and things that reactivate our negative patterns, we can either steer clear of them or be prepared to deal with them differently.

The better we know ourselves, the better we are able to manage ourselves and support our positive patterns.

## BUTTERFLY ON MY SHOULDER

Exercising this kind of vigilance doesn't have to be difficult or unpleasant. I learned to do it from a teacher who told me about carrying a butterfly around on my shoulder. He said that I should go through my days as if there were a gentle and all-seeing butterfly on my shoulder that watched everything I thought, did, and said: the fair witness.

So I imagined a blue iridescent butterfly sitting on my shoulder who would observe how I thought about my family, my work, and my home. It would listen to the tone of voice I used with various people in my life, and observe what kinds of things upset me.

The butterfly on my shoulder helped me become aware of how I was going about my daily living and where I was choosing to concentrate my energies—to see myself as I went through my day. The idea was not to beat myself up; that would just be another form of personal negativity. The butterfly would enable me to better know my triggers for the unwanted thoughts and actions. That was information I needed if I wanted to begin healing myself. If I didn't know what the problem was, how could I heal it?

Whenever I wasn't sure how the negativity was operating within me, I would just sit quietly for a few moments. It was amazing how quickly I began to spot—through the butterfly's eyes—my self-sabotaging attitudes. Whenever I saw something I wanted to change, I would intentionally relive it mentally in its ideal form. That gave me the map I needed to move forward toward my new destination.

# Chapter 13

## *BUILDING STEADY ATTITUDES: MORE TECHNIQUES*

Making the commitment to heal personal negativity and embarking on a positive program of mental and emotional care is an important step in building a new life based on dynamically proactive love, health, and optimism.

You will probably notice some results right away. They may be big things like a new job or relationship, or small things like having more energy in the morning, enjoying your time with the kids more, or not getting so upset in traffic. Some days, your new mental care orientation will seem like something magical that has utterly transformed your life. Other days, life may not feel too different from the way it's always been.

Remember, making these kinds of dramatic and permanent changes takes time. Changes involving the habits of a lifetime don't usually happen overnight (although you shouldn't rule out that possibility). What you're after is a daily letting go of stress, followed by nourishment.

The following are techniques and exercises to remember. Some may seem a little silly, but that's fine—you can think of them as tricks for change. All of them are designed to work along with your concentrated, twenty-minute Mind Fitness program, and to help build steady attitudes.

### THE "REMEMBER" SIGN

I have a friend in Hawaii who has a huge banner strung across his living room. It says REMEMBER. It reminds him to be conscious of choosing his attitudes and his actions, rather than reacting automatically based on the habits from the past.

Remembering—being mindful that we are the ones who choose what we do, say, and feel—is the cornerstone of building steady attitudes. One symptom is being resistant to really owning that knowledge all the time. We need to remember that we are in the driver's seat every moment of every day. We need to be aware of where our weak spots and negative tendencies are, so that we can watch out for them and begin to heal them. That's easier if we also remember our higher self: the part of us that loves, grows, and is in balance.

Whenever I entered my friend's house, I felt calm and peaceful. Remembering to remember always brought me home within myself.

### NEGATIVITY BREAKERS

These techniques help break the habit and accustomed energy of negative thinking, and refocus that energy toward building a habit of more self-supportive and expansive thinking. When we begin healing negativity, it's a lot like cleaning house. We throw away things that are no longer useful or enjoyable, and replace them with new things that have more meaning to us now. (See the visualization of Emptying Your Mental Closet in chapter 12.)

In this case, we're throwing away old thoughts and patterns of thinking. We're also doing some renovating and redecorating with thought patterns that are loving, optimistic, and open to success in all areas. We may want to knock out some walls, add some new doors or windows, or even build on a few new rooms with Mind Fitness.

I call the following techniques "Negativity Breakers" because they act like electrical circuit breakers to cut off the energy to old, negative habits. Most are physical actions that can be done simply to stop the flow of whatever is happening at the moment. After the negative flow has stopped, we can turn our attention to replacing it with something personally beneficial. Remember, you do not want to deny your feelings but you do want to move the energy to be more constructive.

When you find yourself succumbing to negativity, try one of these Negativity Breakers to actively change the direction of your physical and mental energy:

**Shake your hands** really hard, as if you were shaking off water droplets. As you shake your hands, visualize negativity flying off your fingertips and away from you. This exercise is amazingly effective for breaking up the tension and heaviness that is a symptom of negativity. It's like smashing a thin layer of ice on a pail of water.

**Move your body.** Often the physical act of moving your body will also move things around in your mind. When you start going down the negative road, get yourself into motion. Take a walk. Stretch. Turn on the music, dance, do anything that changes your energy.

You may find at first that your body doesn't want to move, or that it wants to move in ways that are small and stilted. Give yourself a few minutes and watch the changes. Your movements will take on breadth, shape, and rhythm, and so will your thinking!

Your internal chemistry actually changes as your body becomes more free, animated, and alive. These physiological changes cause psychological changes, and can move you out of the depression.

**"No!"** Another version of the Stop and Cancel refocus-

s

ing exercise, this technique is rather dramatic, and very effective. It also combines movement and words to state that you are no longer willing to accept the old obsessive negativity in your life. When you catch yourself thinking something negative, take a stand and say out loud to yourself as you lower your hands in a cutting gesture, "No! I will not accept that self-destructive thought anymore! I replace it with . . . [here say your chosen replacement]."

There is nothing wrong with being dramatic. It usually works best. This technique underscores your own power to *reject* self-destructive habits, while creating new ones. Again, I want to emphasize that you are not to deny your negative inner feelings, but I believe that the kind of deep psychotherapy that digs up and expresses these may not always be needed to correct negative attitudes and reactions. The power of self-imposed, constructive denial can also be a healing force, especially when you find yourself barreling forward on a train that you have looked at carefully and decided that you no longer want to ride. Stop that train any way you can and deny its power over you. This dramatic "*No!*" accompanied by a hand motion can work well with children and teenagers when you just want to stop the flow of negative or abusive energy with attention-getting drama.

**Smile.** It sounds crazy—as if you are pushing your deep inner feelings away—but again, you are using this technique when something has been identified, acknowledged, and accepted, yet still remains obsessive within your behavioral pattern. You want to rechannel your habitual reactive energy flow. If you can smile even when you don't want to, often you can change the focus of the thought. You may have to force the corners of your mouth up, stretch your cheeks back, and struggle a bit to make it look like a real smile, but the results are amazing. If you find this difficult, think of it not as a smile but as a facial expression. Something in making those physical movements actually changes the way we think and feel. This is an extreme example of "fake it and you'll make it," but it can often work to redirect the automatic negative response.

**Talk happy.** This really sounds silly, but try it. It is another version of "fake it and you'll make it." When you are feeling down or depressed, try making liberal use of positive, happy words: "Yes, like, love, wonderful, happy, peaceful, fun, energizing, successful, good." You are taking charge of your negativity.

This won't be easy; your ego will fight you. It helps to prepare beforehand. Sit down some time when you are feeling great and make a list of positive words, so that you can pull it out when you don't feel so great and they aren't exactly on the tip of your tongue. Again, it sounds silly, but not as silly as rejecting an idea that works, or living your life self-destructively.

**Reserve negative comments.** When someone comes up with an idea, don't jump all over it. Adopt a personal guideline that you will brainstorm about any idea for several minutes without anyone making any negative comments. Think of it as keeping a ball up in the air for a few minutes. See if the idea has some merit as you "bounce it around" before you reject it entirely. It may be better than it first appears, or certain parts of it may be useful even if others are not. The important thing is that you will be teaching yourself to slow down your reactions.

**Take a deep breath.** This is a classic, used a great deal in Eastern practices. When things aren't going well, taking a deep breath not only serves as a reminder that situations can be turned around, but helps break up the energy, relaxes you, and sends a fresh supply of oxygen to your brain. Many people began using this technique for the physical benefits—relaxation and oxygenation—and found that they developed a positive pattern and association with it. Now when they take a deep breath, they not only get the physical benefits, but associate the action with more positive outcomes and automatically move into a more expansive frame of mind.

**Find and use a personal success symbol.** Allow your creativity to be inspired. Use a picture, a little drawing, a symbol of some kind—just something visual that you associate with clear self-directed intentions of personal success to remind you to focus on moving into that frame of mind.

One woman in a group reported that when she stopped smoking, she went out and bought a sheet of little stickers in the shape of red apples. She stuck them up in various places in her house to remind her of that success and of the fact that if she could give up smoking, she could do anything. She associated the apple with the tale of William Tell splitting the apple on top of the boy's head. As a child, she'd been impressed by this impossible feat. She put the stickers on her bathroom mirror, refrigerator, desk lamp, computer, telephone, and nightstand. Whenever she saw those little red apples, she was reminded of a seemingly impossible feat—and that she was actually succeeding in that impossibility. She was reminded that she was doing this for herself, and she acknowledged the self-esteem she had gained from the victory. She began to feel that she was carrying that energy into other life areas as well.

**Acknowledge other people.** Whether it's an appreciation card to a coworker, a birthday message to a distant cousin, an "I love you" note to a parent or sibling, a thank-you to the guy with jumper cables who helped you start your car at midnight, or a letter of appreciation to be placed in someone's personnel file, letting other people know you appreciate them makes *you* feel good, too. It taps into that spirit of generosity, begins an upward spiral of energy, and comes back to you in mysterious ways.

**Do a mini-visualization.** The meeting is in five minutes. Suddenly you feel unprepared and panicked. You've done your homework, but somehow doubt overwhelms you and it seems as if everything is going to go wrong. You don't have time to sit down, close your eyes, and do a full-scale visualization, but you can take a deep breath, close your eyes for ten seconds, and get a picture of success.

Your quick mind lift might have you spin through the entire meeting on fast forward, or just get a sense of how you want things to feel while it's going on, or envision what you want the final result to be.

Putting the meeting back in your mind's eye, bringing it into your own mental sphere, is a reminder that you don't have to be afraid. Blast the whole situation with positive energy, lean back, and let your positive attitudes take over.

### KINDNESS TO OURSELVES

Building steady attitudes happens in two phases:
- breaking the old, negative patterns, and
- replacing them with new, more self-chosen ways of thinking and acting

Being actively kind to ourselves is part of the second phase. Most of us have not been brought up to take gentle, loving care of ourselves. We've been discouraged from pampering ourselves; we were taught that such behavior is either selfish or a waste of time. But actively nourishing our souls and being gentle with our bodies demonstrates that we care about ourselves, and that we want to replace some of the harsh treatment with kindness.

We can be kind to ourselves in many ways: physical, emotional, and spiritual. The first step is to treat ourselves with more understanding and acceptance. We are human beings, and have human frailties. None of us is perfect, and it's not realistic to demand perfection of ourselves. We need to be as gentle and loving about our own flaws as we are about the flaws of someone we love.

Another step is to give ourselves *permission to do things that feel good*—walking in the sunshine, sitting down with a cup of tea, watching a comedy on TV, stroking a child's hair, or simply sitting quietly doing nothing. Most of us don't give ourselves permission to do these things simply because we want to do them. We walk because it's good exercise, we drink the tea because we need a rest so we can get back to work, we watch the comedy because it's what the family is doing that night, we stroke the child's hair because we're taking care of him or her. We need to calm down, stop thinking about what we should be doing all the time, and become aware of doing things just for the pleasure of doing them. That is called living in the present moment.

Negativity often takes a physical form when we don't take good care of ourselves—whether by eating poorly, not getting adequate exercise, or just generally being mentally and emotionally out of balance with ourselves. One of the themes of this book is that an attitude can be *learned* rather than just *passively caught*. Depriving ourselves of love and nurturing is a good way to keep the cycle of illness and negativity going. It shows up in little ways. How do we put on hand cream or brush our teeth? How fast do we eat? Do we stop to taste and enjoy our food? These are all little indications to ourselves of how much— or how little—we are gentle and caring with ourselves.

We're often so busy and hurried that we don't realize how harsh and demanding we are. We don't even stop to consider what it would look like if we did treat ourselves with more kindness and consideration.

I used to do training for grammar school teachers on being kind to themselves. When they began to treat *themselves* more gently, amazing things started to happen in their classrooms. They began to treat the children with more gentleness as well. They demanded less perfection, and they were more caring and respectful with the children. When we give ourselves permission to be more restful and gentle, we give that same permission to others. Once we begin the process, the cycle of kindliness and respect feeds off itself.

**Story:** A group participant told us, "I became aware of how ungentle I was with myself one day when a friend who was a hair stylist was cutting my hair. Before we started, she asked me to brush it. She watched, and after a moment stopped me and said, "Look at the way you're brushing your hair. You're not being very gentle or caring with yourself. You're not loving yourself very much."

"I was stunned. I stopped brushing and realized that she was right. I was tugging and pulling at my hair in a very unthinking and nongentle manner. I realized that this was how I treated myself in many areas of life. That moment of realization opened up a whole new path for me. It was the beginning of being more actively loving with myself, and therefore with others. I started moving a bit more slowly and gently, taking the time to brush my hair instead of attacking it. I began to see other parts of my life where I could treat myself with more kindness. Instead of taking showers, I started taking baths more frequently, enjoying the time I was actively caring for myself. I gave myself permission to engage in my hobbies more often, to spend more time with my family, to sit by the fire in the evening, and to enjoy other simple pleasures. Each year, I am learning to give myself more permission to be kind to myself and honor the higher self within me. What I am really learning is that it is a continual process."

Being kind to ourselves on all levels is one of the most important things we can do to build our steady attitudes. It is a conscious act, and one that is essential for healing. As we are more nurturing with ourselves, we become more considerate and kinder to other people. We have fewer judgments and more compassion. It's easier to see what it would feel like to be in the other person's position. We develop more genuine affection for people, and so we enjoy them more. We begin a cycle of love that nurtures all of us—and there is nothing like love to turn a negative filter into a positive one. That is where giving and receiving start to blend together.

## SPIRITUAL NURTURING

We deeply need to nurture ourselves on a spiritual level. Treating ourselves to a gift now and then, taking a long weekend, reading a good book, saying "No" to another obligation, taking time out to do a sport or activity that we like—all these things nourish us on the physical and mental planes. Nurturing our souls adds a whole new and critically important dimension to our personal life journeys. It means taking the time to appreciate our connection with the infinite, with the mysterious, with nature, and with everything around us.

We may simply admire a flower or watch a stream as it flows downhill, or watch the sun sink into the ocean. If you're in a city, you may watch a raindrop on the window, see a tree overhead, or imagine connecting with people on a heart level while walking down the street. We direct ourselves to see over the personality self, the racial self, the economic and job-related self, and extend to others in a new and more eternal way. The soul naturally comes to life when we consciously stop to realize our connection with something larger than ourselves, and remind ourselves that we are part of a greater whole. As we stop to connect with the mystery of all of life in *all* its various and amazing forms, living for centuries on this planet, all doing the same biological things in some many diverse ways, we tap into an awe that begins to help us overcome our own little personalities and touch that deeper, more eternal part of our own selves.

There are many, many forms of inner quieting and meditation; only you will know which is best for you. You may choose a formal method that has been taught for centuries, or you may choose simply to sit quietly with yourself for a few minutes each day focusing on inner calm and peace. No form of meditation is better than another. What counts is the peace, energy, and love that you find within yourself as a result.

Meditation is a time to be quietly with your deeper self and to connect with the infinite, God, a higher power, or whatever you like to call the force that brings us all into being and binds us all together. It is a place where you find grace, where you can just let things be and appreciate them as they are. Enjoying a meal is nourishment for the body. Reading or engaging in a challenging conversation is nourishment for the mind. Meditating or inwardly silencing yourself is nourishment for the soul. It is the essence of any personal Mind Fitness program.

When you first sit down to spend this quiet time with yourself, you may find that all your attention is on your body. You may feel tension in various spots, and need to do some deep abdominal breathing in order to release it.

When your body has relaxed, simply move inside and begin to quiet your mind, slowly asking it to relinquish its chatter and just be still. Try repeating a word or phrase that has personal meaning to you. This may be a formal mantra given to you by a teacher, or some word such as "Peace" that you repeat over and over until your mind becomes quiet. Each time your attention wanders, gently bring it back to the word. Don't beat yourself up if you get distracted. This is an exercise in forgiveness and acceptance.

The easist and best way to quiet the mind is just to watch your breathing. Be aware of each breath as it enters and leaves your lower abdomen. You may want to count the breaths or see the stream of air as a color.

Another good way to quiet a chattering mind is to imagine yourself sitting by the edge of a pond or river, resting as the sun and the quieting forces of nature work their magic on you. You may have a template visualization that you use to move into a relaxed state.

When the body and mind are finally at peace, simply rest and allow yourself to merge with your concept of the infinite. At this point, I feel a great richness pour over me like honey and there seems to be no difference between my inside and my outside. I feel at one with myself and with everything else. There is no movement or chatter.

The more I practice meditation and inner quieting, the better it feels and the more centered and calm I become in my daily life. I feel more integrated on all levels: physical, mental, emotional, and spiritual.

Meditation doesn't have to be anything mystical. It is simply a time each day for centering, quietness, and relaxation of body and mind, a time for making contact with the subtle parts of yourself and reminding yourself that you are connected with all of life. It is the inner listening part of Mind Fitness. The quieting allows the intuition to take form within your conscious mind.

Explore various types of inner quieting, or make up a meditation for yourself, and practice a few minutes a day. You will notice a difference, and it will enhance the focusing work you do with the more active parts of Mind Fitness.

### SELF-ACKNOWLEDGMENT

Acknowledgment is a positive force, whether directed toward others or ourselves. There can rarely be too much of it. Self-acknowledgment or praise is not something we are taught when we are young, so you may need some practice. You may need to make a conscious effort at first to seek out your good deeds, good thoughts, and good attitudes, and inwardly praise yourself for developing and nurturing them.

Most of us have had to work to develop the positive aspects of our lives, and we deserve credit and acknowledgment. Praise is the best way to make things grow. If we want more positive thoughts, words, and actions in our lives, we need to build on what we already have by acknowledging and praising the ones that are already there.

Another aspect of acknowledgment is to become more aware of moments that are especially fulfilling, appreciate them, and build upon them. We need to take time out to highlight those times, and the people with whom we share them. It's usually much easier to be critical and judge what isn't working than it is to seek out the positive, especially in ourselves. The inability to compliment ourselves and others is a clear symptom of lack of self-appreciation . . . another cornerstone of personal negativity.

If acknowledgment of yourself or others is difficult for you, practice by imagining yourself in a situation in which you are doing it. Concentrate on the images of praise, and on the reactions you get. In your mind, imagine and live how you respond to the words. How do others respond when you acknowledge them? What is the ultimate result of the praise you give them and yourself? Do all this in your imagination as you shift from being one person to another.

Acknowledgment and criticism both are habits. Since it is the nature of human beings to put attention on ourselves, we will probably have one habit or the other, depending on how we view ourselves. Since we can make a choice, it better serves us to choose acknowledgment. As part of the personal negativity pattern, we're often quick to criticize ourselves, but much slower to acknowledge a goal achieved, an attitude changed, or a more positive frame of mind. Sometimes we work for years toward something, and hardly even bother to compliment ourselves once we have achieved it.

Recognizing the higher and more positive aspects of ourselves is a key to personal development. We need strokes in order to grow, and we don't want to always count on getting them from other people. Part of becoming self-determined is learning to provide them for ourselves, and to have fun doing it. Developing the habit of acknowledging yourself in a healthy manner goes a long way toward replacing the habit of self-criticism, and is an important part of exchanging the negative filter for a positive one.

## MIND LIFTS

Remember mind lifts—those brief sessions of "pumping images" that we can do several times in the course of a day? Mind lifts are like lifts done with weights in the gym. They are brief repetitions that *build attitudinal muscles* and shape them to fit our visions. We can "lift" these whenever we think about it and want to take a hand in shaping our lives. Mind lifts help us work toward our goals, and keep our energy and focus where we want them to be—whether that means pushing our level of enthusiasm a little higher, or letting ourselves relax into a quiet time.

We can use images of goals achieved, relationships appreciated, love in bloom, happiness enjoyed, even the good fortune of sunshine . . . anything we want. The important thing is to feel the feelings. Some examples:

**Images of Happiness:** Most of us have never taken the time to consider what our lives would actually look and feel like if we were completely happy. During one of your meditation or Mind Fitness sessions, visualize yourself as a totally happy, completely fulfilled person. What would you be doing? Who would you be with? How would you feel? What would you look like? What would you be wearing? What would your attitudes be? What would your life look like? Really feel how you would be.

Once you have a clear picture of what total happiness might look and feel like to you, you can flash on it as a mind lift at any time and bring it closer to reality.

**Images of Love:** Now create some images of love. It can be romantic love, the love of friendship, family love, any and all kinds of love you choose. Who is there with you? How do you feel? What do you want for this person? For yourself? What is the texture of your relationship? Where is it going? What are the results of your love in both of your lives?

**Images of Job Fulfillment:** Do the same type of mental play, but this time focus on what you would ideally like to see happen in your job. It can be a paid job, a volunteer job, or the job of being a mate, parent, or caregiver to an elderly relative. What are the basic demands of the job situation and how are you handling them? Who is with you? What kind of an attitude do you have? How much self-acknowledgment are you giving yourself? How much acknowledgment do you ideally want from your coworkers?

Make up your own mind lifts for work, sports, artistic endeavors, health, any area in which you want to grow. Use them frequently. Remember, attitudes are like muscles. They only stay strong and healthy when they are used *and exercised.*

### A WAY OF LIFE

Learning to build steady attitudes, like sticking with a regular fitness program, takes patience and perseverance. Inner mind work and self-direction is not just an exercise we do for a few minutes by ourselves each day. The goal is to make the new, positive habits a way of life. Building steady attitudes means that regardless of the daily ups and downs, we endeavor to hold ourselves on an even keel that is basically upbeat and generous, not falling prey to abrupt shifts in mood or long depressions. We stay awake and aware.

We focus on life's opportunities because we have chosen to have a new consciousness, a new way of relating to life. The classic test of whether you're an optimist or a pessimist asks whether you see a glass of water as half full or half empty. Which way do you choose to go through life? We always have the choice. We can make optimism as natural a response as pessimism may be for us today, if we choose optimism every day.

As we go through life, each of us will encounter some severe "downdrafts." We can't control events outside ourselves, but we *do* have the ability to choose how we feel about those events, and how we react to them. How we feel at any given moment has less to do with external events than it does with *how we relate to ourselves* and the attitudes we foster within ourselves. Often it is the people who have had little hardship in their lives who have the most negative and self-indulgent attitudes—who see the glass as half-empty—while others, who have had to survive grave life difficulties, have come to terms with darkness and learned to focus on that half-full glass of water. When our point of concentration becomes *internal*, rather than *external*, we gain power over our own lives.

## PERSONAL TO GLOBAL COMMITMENT

The positive orientation of healthier people ripples out from individuals, to families, to communities, to nations, and to the world. It is a natural evolution in consciousness. It is the next place for us to go. It is only a matter of time before more and more human beings embrace the expansive power of their minds as they interrelate with their bodies and with others.

Imagine the potential of six billion people free to construct dreams, goals, and visions, to imagine the very best for themselves and the rest of the world, everyone participating in a compassionate and mentally healthy form of thinking and consciousness.

Imagine what relationships among people and nations would be like. People would be free to express the deep connection and love that have always been there, but have been clouded by fear and separation. We would truly become the family of humankind caring for ourselves, each other, and the Earth on which we live.

I am always amazed at how quickly we humans respond to the positive. I was reminded of this by a documentary on Mother Theresa. The incident occurred years ago but it still has such power today. A boy in Beirut had been so shell-shocked that his entire soul seemed to have retreated deep within his body. He just lay on his side shaking, completely unresponsive to anything, staring with eyes empty from the horror he had seen around him. Mother Theresa simply started to stroke this boy's head and back and, incredibly, within just a few minutes he had stopped shaking and turned his eyes and hand toward the source of this loving touch. I was astonished that a person so deeply contracted would respond so quickly to a simple loving touch.

We all have been shell-shocked by our own personal battles and we all respond to the positive. We have the ability to touch ourselves and one another in this same way with our love. A smile heals like sunlight. As we begin to grow and actively empower ourselves by using a personal Mind Fitness program, that smile gets closer to the surface—more available both to us and to the people around us.

I believe that those of us who live relatively free of persecution, abject poverty, and constant physical danger have the responsibility to pioneer and actively support this next step in human evolution and consciousness. We are the ones privileged to turn our minds and hearts first to our own healing and growth, and then to reach out to our neighbors in compassion and justice.

Once we have moved beyond our own emotional and physical survival, we can turn our creativity toward the task of contributing to others in whatever our chosen path may be. The desire to love and contribute to one another is a primal human urge. The commitment to consciously design our life around compassion and love is a personal commitment, to ourselves and to others. It might mean something as simple as devoting a few minutes a day to imaging yourself and the world at peace, or to imaging a change of understanding that allows us humans to overcome selfishness and to live together on this planet in respect and justice.

> The possible human is inclined toward fairness, goodness and excellence. When we create enough individuals so inclined, we then create societies capable of fairness, goodness and excellence.
>
> James Comer, Yale University

# Recommended Books

I have found these books to be very helpful and enjoyable:

*The Art of Happiness: A Handbook for Living.* His Holiness the Dalai Lama and Howard C. Cutler, M.D. Riverhead Books.

*Beyond the Relaxation Response: How to Harness the Healing Power of Your Personal Beliefs.* Herbert Benson, M.D., and William Proctor. Berkley Publishing Group.

*Change Your Mind, Change Your Life: Concepts in Attitudinal Healing.* Gerald G. Jampolsky, M.D., and Diane V. Cirincione. Bantam Books.

*Creative Imagery: How to Visualize in All Five Senses.* William Fezler, Ph.D. Simon & Schuster.

*Creative Visualization.* Shakti Gawain. Bantam Books.

*Emotional Intelligence: Why It Can Matter More than IQ.* Daniel P. Goleman. Bantam Books.

*Fire in the Soul: A New Psychology of Spiritual Optimism.* Joan Borysenko. Warner Books.

*The Healer Within: The New Medicine of Mind and Body.* Steven Locke, M.D., and Douglas Colligan. Dutton/Plume.

*Imagery in Healing: Shamanism & Modern Medicine.* Jeanne Achterberg. Shambhala Publications.

*Living Simply Through the Day: Spiritual Survival in a Complex Age.* Tilden Edwards. Paulist Press.

*Love and Will*. Rollo May. Delta.

*Love Is Letting Go of Fear*. Gerald G. Jampolsky. Celestial Arts Publishing Company.

*The Miracle of Mindfulness: A Manual on Meditation*. Thich Nhat Hanh, translated by Mobi Ho. Beacon Press.

*Myths to Live By*. Joseph Campbell. Viking Penguin Books.

*The Relaxation Response*. Herbert Benson, M.D. with Miriam Z. Klipper. Wholecare.

*The Relaxation & Stress Reduction Workbook*. Martha Davis. New Harbinger.

*Sabbath: Restoring the Sacred Rhythm of Rest & Delight*. Wayne Muller. Bantam Books.

*The Seat of the Soul*. Gary Zukav. Simon & Schuster.

*Toward a Psychology of Being*. Abraham H. Maslow, Ph.D. John Wiley & Sons.

*Wishing Well: Making Your Every Wish Come True*. Paul Pearsall. Hyperion.

*Your Maximum Mind*. Herbert Benson, M.D., and William Proctor. Times Books.

TS